And the Word Became Flesh

And the Word Became Flesh

And Dwelt Among Us

Holly Hoffman Thomas

RESOURCE *Publications* • Eugene, Oregon

AND THE WORD BECAME FLESH
And Dwelt Among Us

Copyright © 2018 Holly Hoffman Thomas. All rights reserved. Except for brief quotations in critical publications or reviews, no part of this book may be reproduced in any manner without prior written permission from the publisher. Write: Permissions, Wipf and Stock Publishers, 199 W. 8th Ave., Suite 3, Eugene, OR 97401.

Resource Publications
An Imprint of Wipf and Stock Publishers
199 W. 8th Ave., Suite 3
Eugene, OR 97401

www.wipfandstock.com

PAPERBACK ISBN: 978-1-5326-4726-0
HARDCOVER ISBN: 978-1-5326-4727-7
EBOOK ISBN: 978-1-5326-4728-4

Manufactured in the U.S.A.

All Scripture References are taken from the New American Bible, Revised Edition; St. Joseph Edition, copyright 2010 by the Confraternity of Christian Doctrine, Inc., Washington, DC, U.S.A. Used by permission.

All Catechism References are from the English translation of the Catechism of the Catholic Church, Second Edition, for the United States of America, copyright 1994 by the United States Catholic Conference, Inc. Used by permission.

All Saint Quotes are taken from www.AZQuotes.com

Chapter 2 Picture has been in my possession for 25+ years now. The artist is unknown.

Chapter 3 Song "City on Our Knees" by tobymac Copyright 2009 by Capital CMG Publishing. Used by permission.

Chapter 7 Prayer: Prayer of Saint Francis by Saint Francis. Used by permission.

Chapter 8 Song "Take Me In" by Dave Browning. Used by permission.

Chapter 9 Prayer: Footprints by Mary Stevenson Copyright 1936. Used by permission.

Chapter 12 Song "Speak Life" by tobymac Copyright 2012 by Capital CMG Publishing. Used by Permission.

Dedicated
In Memory of
Dad Thomas

A greater man I have never known. It was enough.
I love you, Dad Thomas. Forever.

Dedicated
In Memory of
Grandma Hoffman

Remember all the days we talked about how we thought my daily suffering was because you would live to be 100 years old? Well, Grandma, it's ok you didn't live that long. God's ways are beyond our understanding. Thank you for the memories.
I love you, Grandma. Forever.

Contents

List of Illustrations, Tables, and Song Lyrics | x
Acknowledgements | xi
Introduction | xiii

Part 1—Theological Virtues | 1
1. Faith | 3
2. Hope | 7
3. Charity | 13

Part 2—Cardinal Virtues | 25
4. Prudence | 27
5. Justice | 32
6. Fortitude | 39
7. Temperance | 44

Part 3—Human Virtues Close to my Heart | 51
8. Patience | 53
9. Compassion | 61
10. Perseverance | 69
11. Authenticity | 74
12. Purposefulness | 82

Appendix 1: Lincoln's "Failures"? | 89
Appendix 2: Emancipation Proclamation Text | 91
Bibliography | 95

Illustrations, Tables, and Song Lyrics

Image	Don't EVER give up!	8
Song Lyrics	"City on our Knees"	22
Song Lyrics	"Take Me In"	59
Image	Saint Monica	71
Chart	Definitions of Terms for Authenticity	76
Image	Jesus Divine Mercy	85
Song Lyrics	"Speak Life"	86

Acknowledgements

Mommy—With heartfelt gratitude, I thank you, Mommy, for your daily optimistic encouragement. Your words are embedded in my heart. Thank you for reading each chapter gaining insight into how God's Words have gifted me immensely. You are the most influential Catholic Christian in my life: now and forever. As our bond strengthens, know that I look up to you as a prime example of God's love for all. I will always love you.

Scotty—As days turn to months turn to years, I love you more with each passing day. No matter the circumstances, you have never let me down. Our sacramental marriage bond cemented as one strengthens me daily. You complete me; make me whole. I love you more than words can say.

Introduction

As my teacher began class with the sign of the cross, each student quieted and sat in the closest chair available. At the end of Opening Prayer, my teacher scanned the room, locking eyes with each student. This alone captured each student's attention. In barely a whisper, the teacher asked, "Who among you wishes to be a saint?". As I slowly raised my hand, I was aware that only two other students also raised their hands.

My teacher went on to explain that yes, you too can become a saint. You may not be canonized and have your name scribed in the Catholic books with the great, well known saints of ole, but yes, you can become a saint.

Using this concept of becoming a saint, I entitled my book "And the Word was Made Flesh; And Dwelt Among Us". The Word is GOD. God became flesh in the form of Jesus. Through Jesus, God dwells among us. We, too, must dwell "among" one another and choose conquering with kindness as the means of communication.

The key to becoming a saint is to actively practice the virtues. How can you practice the virtues if you do not understand the concept of "virtues"? This book is comprised of twelve virtues that will aid you in your quest to become a saint. The three theological virtues (faith, hope, charity) are in Part 1 of this book. Next, you will dive into the four cardinal virtues (prudence, justice, fortitude, temperance). Finally, you will learn about five virtues close to my heart (patience, compassion, perseverance, authenticity, purposefulness). It is my hope that you will find at least one of these virtues

Introduction

tugging at your heart to develop further in your life. Perhaps learning of these virtues will lead you to research other virtues and their meaning to you.

In a concise, easy to follow format, each chapter consists of the following elements pertaining to each virtue:

- Definition
- Scripture Passages
- Catechism of the Catholic Church References
- A Saint that exhibits the virtue
- Real Lives, Real Stories connecting each virtue to another person
- Reflection tying the saint to the other person as he/she strives for that virtue
- Questions to guide you to reflect on each virtue
- Digging Deeper where you can ponder Biblical figures and how they practice each virtue
- Closing Prayer

As you journey through this book, I pray you grow closer to God. Let us stand together to live a virtuous life, countercultural to what the world offers today.

Part 1

Theological Virtues
Faith
Hope
Charity

New American Bible Revised Edition

Galatians 5:22-23
"In contrast, the fruit of the Spirit is love, joy, peace, patience, kindness, generosity, faithfulness, gentleness, self-control. Against such there is no law."

Catechism of the Catholic Church

#1840
"The theological virtues dispose Christians to live in a relationship with the Holy Trinity. They have God for their origin, their motive, and their object—God known by faith, God hoped in and loved for his own sake."

#1841
"There are three theological virtues: faith, hope, and charity. They inform all the moral virtues and give life to them."

Chapter 1

Faith

Defined in my own Words: deep realization that God will care for you
Scripture:

> *Matthew 17:19-21*
> "Then the disciples approached Jesus in private and said, "Why could we not drive it out?" He said to them, "Because of your little faith. Amen, I say to you, if you have faith the size of a mustard seed, you will say to this mountain, 'Move from here to there,' and it will move. Nothing will be impossible for you."

Catechism of the Catholic Church:

> *#1842*
> "By faith, we believe in God and believe all that he has revealed to us and that Holy Church proposes for our belief."

Sponsored by: Saint Mother Teresa of Calcutta
Patron Saint of: World Youth Day
Feast Day: September 5
Insight in Saint Mother Teresa's Words:

> "We can do no great things, Only small things with great Love" "Unless life is lived for others, it is not worthwhile."

Part 1: Theological Virtues

"Prayer is nothing but that oneness with Christ. As Scripture says in St. Paul, 'I live no longer, but Christ lives in me.' Christ prays in me, Christ thinks in me, Christ looks through my eyes, Christ speaks through my words. Christ works with my hands, Christ walks with my feet, Christ loves with my heart."

Real Lives, Real Stories:

One wonders at times how God works all for good. During these times, there are friends in our lives. The truest of true friends stand by your side through it all, whether personalities are similar or different. Each friendship is interwoven with God's loving touch.

Saint Mother Teresa of Calcutta and Princess Diana of Wales were polar opposites, yet they were actually close friends. Mother Teresa owned next to nothing, in which the entirety of her belongings could fit in a child sized backpack. She is the perfect example of living countercultural to what the world offers. In contrast, Princess Diana had everything humanly made at her fingertips, the luxury of all luxuries. Yet, there are pictures of the two together holding hands, hugging, and smiling. Though we may never know the depth of their friendship, the following shows both of their hearts going out to those without a voice.

Princess Diana helped Mother Teresa found a shelter for pregnant women who wanted to adopt their children out rather than abort them because they could not take care of the babies themselves. Who knows how many countless pregnant women saved the lives of their babies after being ministered to by Mother Teresa and/or Princess Diana? Princess Diana provided the monetary support to start this program in this house in Calcutta, India, and visited frequently. Mother Teresa sheltered these women not only with a place to live, but also with love.

Little did we know this friendship must continue in Heaven, as Mother Teresa followed Princess Diana to Heaven six days later in September 1997. So, I leave you with this. The moral of the story of these friends is that no matter where you come from, love is in

Faith

your heart. If your heart finds a compassionate place to give, I urge you to act on it. After all, God does have plans for you.

Reflection:

You might wonder why I chose Saint Mother Teresa of Calcutta as the sponsor for the virtue of faith beings that one of the most prolific quotes is attributed to her: "we do no great things, only small things with great love". The reason is simple. Mother Teresa had faith the size of a mustard seed.

Daily prayer sustained Saint Mother Teresa. She attuned her ear in God's direction. She didn't just listen to God's direction; most importantly she took action on what God had asked her to do. One task entrusted to Saint Mother Teresa was to found the Missionaries of Charity, rooted in India. Her ministry focused on ministering to the poorest of the poor; many of whom no one loved. She also opened a pro-life home filled with women who chose adoption for their children versus abortion.

With complete, unadulterated faith in God, Saint Mother Teresa looked at each person, eye to eye, and saw the face of Jesus in each one. Not only that, but Saint Mother Teresa took it a step further: expressing with words God's unending love for each one. This resulted in a majority of those she ministered to accept Jesus in their hearts. Dare I try to emulate Saint Mother Teresa by seeing Jesus in EVERYONE I meet? This is possible for you as well. All that is required is a deep abiding faith in God the size of a mustard seed. This, coupled with trusting Him to guide us in our every endeavor, our faith will soon surpass to a greater capacity.

> **Question 1:** How has Saint Mother Teresa's ministry to serve the poorest of the poor, through faith in God, helped you see Jesus in all persons you meet?

Part 1: Theological Virtues

Question 2: In what ways are you completely willing to abandon all to focus on being faithful to what God is asking of you? What will it take for you to make that leap of faith?

Digging Deeper: Argue for or against these Biblical figures exhibiting the virtue of *faith*:

- Paul at the moment of his conversion (Acts 9:1-19)

- Rahab hiding the spies (Joshua 6:17-25)

- Sarah upon hearing she would give birth to Isaac (Genesis 17:15-21)

Prayer: God you are like a sunflower. Thank you for changing your look-out to point me in the right direction of my next step. May I always be willing to cross that leap of faith to get to where you have asked me to be. Amen Jesus.

Chapter 2

Hope

Defined in my own Words: continually looking toward the positive in all situations
Scripture:

> *Hebrews 6:11-12*
> "We earnestly desire each of you to demonstrate the same eagerness for the fulfillment of hope until the end, so that you may not become sluggish, but imitators of those who, through faith and patience, are inheriting the promises."

Catechism of the Catholic Church:

> *#1843*
> "By hope we desire, and with steadfast trust await from God, eternal life and the graces to merit it."

Sponsored by: Saint Jude Thaddeaus
Patron Saint of: Lost Causes/Desperate Cases
Feast Day: October 28
Insight in Saint Jude's Words:

> "But you, beloved, build yourselves up in your most holy faith; pray in the holy Spirit. Keep yourselves in the love of God and wait for the mercy of our Lord Jesus Christ that leads to eternal life. On those who waver, have

Part 1: Theological Virtues

mercy; save others by snatching them out of the fire; on others have mercy with fear."

Real Lives, Real Stories:

When I meditate on never giving up, I visualize this:

This cartoon is one of two things that got me through Scotty's DAILY battle of benzodiazepine withdrawal and one nasty side effect from withdrawal: agoraphobia. During this three-year recovery period, you could count on less than one hand those who never gave up hope of Scotty's successful recovery: me and my mom. Day in and day out of 24/7 care, I cried out to God. I asked Saint Jude repetitively to pray for Scotty's recovery. I know without a doubt, Scotty's "hopeless cause/desperate case" resulted in total recovery because of God's amazing grace through the prayers of Saint Jude.

Little by little, Scotty began to see the light as God's healing grace was reaching him through my prayers. As I continued to pray, Scotty began looking for little successes, rather than at the big demon to be conquered. These small successes were getting to Scotty, so much so, that he started praying for himself, finally believing that God would heal him. The more Scotty prayed, the more energized he became to see this demon fall. I was praying 24/7. Saint Jude was praying for Scotty. There were prayers through Scotty's worst periods and prayers of thanks for each little success. Scotty began having days of 'normalcy'. It was during these days of 'normalcy' that Scotty began to see the battle turning in his favor and that with God, he would defeat this demon.

Caring for Scotty 24/7 left me little room to care for myself. Scotty's condition was to the point where I couldn't even leave him while he was sleeping to go to Mass. I knew I needed Jesus in the Eucharist to care for Scotty in this battle. I reached out to the leader in our church in charge of ministry to the sick and homebound. Phil began coming every Saturday afternoon to minister to us. This wasn't just a 5-minute prayer and reception of the Eucharist. Phil genuinely cared for us the first time he set foot in our home. Phil, Scotty, and I chitted the chat about anything and everything. As weeks turned into months turned into three years, Phil's ministry to us at home is what gave Scotty the courage to return to Mass in person when this demon was finally and fully conquered.

Reflection:

There are several expressions to describe the word "hope". Here are five that speak volumes:

> Hope is putting faith to work when doubting would be easier. ~Author Unknown

> Hope is the physician of each misery. ~Irish Proverb

Part 1: Theological Virtues

> Some see a hopeless end, while others see an endless hope. ~Author Unknown
>
> Hope is necessary in every condition. The miseries of poverty, sickness, of captivity, would, without this comfort, be insupportable. ~Samuel Johnson
>
> When the world says, "Give up," Hope whispers, "Try it one more time."~Author Unknown http://www.quotegarden.com/hope.html

The exact reason Saint Jude is chosen as the patron saint of hopeless/desperate cases is not known. What is known is that Saint Jude was one of Jesus' original disciples. He also went by Thaddaeus so as not to confuse him with Judas Iscariot, the ultimate betrayer of Jesus. He was a quiet disciple, with only one verbal passage tied to him in the gospels, which is,

> "Whoever has my commandments and observes them is the one who loves me. And whoever loves me will be loved by my Father, and I will love him and reveal myself to him." Judas, not the Iscariot, said to him, "Master, [then] what happened that you will reveal yourself to us and not to the world?" Jesus answered and said to him, "Whoever loves me will keep my word, and my Father will love him, and we will come to him and make our dwelling with him." John 14:21-23

Saint Jude did write one of the letters in the New Testament. The purpose of this short Letter of Jude is to encourage Christians to gather in faith persevering in the truth that Jesus is our one, true God, and that God loves each of us immensely. We can accomplish this purpose by practicing tolerance. Part of this is evaluating short-term pleasures versus long-term reality. For example, when given a prescription by your doctor, you are to take it according to the doctor's instructions. If you decide to take more than your regular dose to "get high", this is a short-term pleasure that leads to the long-term reality that you will be without your meds until the next refill date authorized by your doctor.

Hope

The crux of the matter is you will be held accountable for these "idols". Contrite confession is necessary to overcome these false gods. Then and only then will you be lifted by God to higher ground.

Question 1: What part of Saint Jude's story do you find most intriguing? Why?

Question 2: Describe a time in your life when you clung to hope.

Digging Deeper: Argue for or against these Biblical figures exhibiting the virtue of *hope*:

- Noah when God made the covenant with him (Genesis 9:1-17)

- Thomas when he cried out, "My Lord and My God" (John 20:24-29)

PART 1: THEOLOGICAL VIRTUES

- John the Baptist in his mother's womb (Luke 1:39-45)

Prayer: Dear Lord Jesus, You are all knowing and all powerful. Remind me during times of 'normalcy' that You are right beside me. Guide me through the rough patches with Your everlasting love. Urge me to cling to You like no other, for it is at all times I shall rely on hope in You, and hope in You alone.

Chapter 3

Charity

Defined in my own Words: choosing to love no matter the circumstances; love in action; sincerely wants what is best for all
Scripture:

> *Exodus 20:1-6*
> "Then God spoke all these words:
> I am the LORD your God, who brought you out of the land of Egypt, out of the house of slavery. You shall not have other gods beside me.[b] You shall not make for yourself an idol or a likeness of anything[c] in the heavens above or on the earth below or in the waters beneath the earth; you shall not bow down before them or serve them. For I, the LORD, your God, am a jealous God, inflicting punishment for their ancestors' wickedness on the children of those who hate me, down to the third and fourth generation[d]; but showing love down to the thousandth generation of those who love me and keep my commandments."

20:3 Beside me: this commandment is traditionally understood as an outright denial of the existence of other gods except the God of Israel; however, in the context of the more general prohibitions in vv. 4–5, v. 3 is, more precisely, God's demand for Israel's exclusive worship and allegiance. The Hebrew phrase underlying the translation "beside me" is, nonetheless, problematic and has been

Part 1: Theological Virtues

variously translated, e.g., "except me," "in addition to me," "in preference to me," "in defiance of me," and "in front of me" or "before my face." The latter translation, with its concrete, spatial nuances, has suggested to some that the prohibition once sought to exclude from the Lord's sanctuary the cult images or idols of other gods, such as the asherah, or stylized sacred tree of life, associated with the Canaanite goddess Asherah (34:13). Over the course of time, as vv. 4–5 suggest, the original scope of v. 3 was expanded.

20:4 Or a likeness of anything: compare this formulation to that found in Dt 5:8, which understands this phrase and the following phrases as specifications of the prohibited idol (Hebrew *pesel*), which usually refers to an image that is carved or hewn rather than cast.

20:5 Jealous: demanding exclusive allegiance. Inflicting punishment...the third and fourth generation: the intended emphasis is on God's mercy by the contrast between punishment and mercy ("to the thousandth generation"—v. 6). Other Old Testament texts repudiate the idea of punishment devolving on later generations (cf. Dt 24:16; Jer 31:29–30; Ez 18:2–4). Yet it is known that later generations may suffer the punishing effects of sins of earlier generations, but not the guilt.

> *Deuteronomy 6:4-6*
> "Hear, O Israel![a] The LORD is our God, the LORD alone! Therefore, you shall love the LORD, your God, with your whole heart, and with your whole being, and with your whole strength. Take to heart these words which I command you today."

a.6:4 Hear, O Israel!: in Hebrew, *shema yisra'el*; hence this passage (vv. 4-9), containing the Great Commandment, is called the Shema. In later Jewish tradition, 11:13-21 and Nm 15:37-41 were added to form a prayer recited every evening and morning. The Lord is our God, the Lord alone: other possible translations are "the Lord our God is one Lord"; "the Lord our God, the Lord is one"; "the Lord is our God, the Lord is one."

Charity

Mark 12:30-32
"You shall love the Lord your God with all your heart, with all your soul, with all your mind, and with all your strength.' The second is this: 'You shall love your neighbor as yourself.' There is no other commandment greater than these." The scribe said to him, "Well said, teacher. You are right in saying, 'He is One and there is no other than he.'"

1 Corinthians 13: 4c-8a
"[a]Love is patient, love is kind. It is not jealous, [love] is not pompous, it is not inflated, it is not rude, it does not seek its own interests, it is not quick-tempered, it does not brood over injury, it does not rejoice over wrongdoing but rejoices with the truth. It bears all things, believes all things, hopes all things, endures all things. [b]Love never fails. If there are prophecies, they will be brought to nothing; if tongues, they will cease; if knowledge, it will be brought to nothing. For we know partially and we prophesy partially, but when the perfect comes, the partial will pass away. When I was a child, I used to talk as a child, think as a child, reason as a child; when I became a man, I put aside childish things. At present we see indistinctly, as in a mirror, but then face to face. At present I know partially; then I shall know fully, as I am fully known. [c]So faith, hope, love remain, these three; but the greatest of these is love."

13:4-7 This paragraph is developed by personification and enumeration, defining love by what it does or does not do. The Greek contains fifteen verbs; it is natural to translate many of them by adjectives in English.

13:8-13 The final paragraph announces its topic, Love never fails. (1 Cor 13:8), then develops the permanence of love in contrast to the charisms (1 Cor 13:9-12), and finally asserts love's superiority even over the other "theological virtues" (1 Cor 13:13).

13:13 In speaking of love, Paul is led by spontaneous association to mention faith and hope as well. They are already a

Part 1: Theological Virtues

well-known triad (cf. 1 Thes 1:3), three interrelated (cf. 1 Cor 13:7) features of Christian life, more fundamental than any particular charism. The greatest. . .is love: love is operative even within the other members of the triad (1 Cor 13:7), so that it has a certain primacy among them. Or, if the perspective is temporal, love will remain (cf. "never fails," 1 Cor 13:8) even when faith has yielded to sight and hope to possession.

> *Colossians 3:12-14*
> "Put on then, as God's chosen ones, holy and beloved, heartfelt compassion, kindness, humility, gentleness, and patience, bearing with one another and forgiving one another, if one has a grievance against another; as the Lord has forgiven you, so must you also do. And over all these put on love, that is, the bond of perfection."

Catechism of the Catholic Church:

> *#1822*
> "Charity is the theological virtue by which we love God above all things for his own sake, and our neighbor as ourselves for the love of God."
>
> *#1823*
> "Jesus makes charity the *new commandment*. [96] By loving his own "to the end," [97] he makes manifest the Father's love which he receives. By loving one another, the disciples imitate the love of Jesus which they themselves receive. Whence Jesus says: "As the Father has loved me, so have I loved you; abide in my love." And again: "This is my commandment, that you love one another as I have loved you." "[98]

[96] Cf. Jn 13:34.
[97] Jn 13:1.
[98] Jn 15:9, 12.

> *#1825*
> "Christ died out of love for us, while we were still "enemies." [100] The Lord asks us to love as he does, even our *enemies*, to make ourselves the neighbor of those farthest

Charity

away, and to love children and the poor as Christ himself. [101]The Apostle Paul has given an incomparable depiction of charity: "charity is patient and kind, charity is not jealous or boastful; it is not arrogant or rude. Charity does not insist on its own way; it is not irritable or resentful; it does not rejoice at wrong, but rejoices in the right. Charity bears all things, believes all things, hopes all things, endures all things." "[102]

[100] Rom 5:10
[101] Cf. Mt 5:44; Lk 10:27-37; Mk 9:37; Mt 25:40, 45.
[102] I Cor 13:4-7.

#1826
"If I ... have not charity," says the Apostle, "I am nothing." Whatever my privilege, service, or even virtue, "if I ... have not charity, I gain nothing." [103] Charity is superior to all the virtues. It is the first of the theological virtues: "So faith, hope, charity abide, these three. But *the greatest of these is charity*." "[104]

[103] I Cor 13:1-4.
[104] I Cor 13:13.

Sponsored by: Saint Therese of Liseiux
Patron Saint of: Missionaries
Feast Day: October 1
Insight in Saint Therese of Liseiux's Words:

"My vocation, at last I have found it; my vocation is love."

"Perfect love means putting up with other peoples shortcomings, feeling no surprise at their weaknesses, finding encouragement even in the slightest evidence of good qualities in them."

Real Lives, Real Stories:

If I had to choose a category of what I want to learn throughout my life, I would choose religious studies. In fact, by continuously studying, I received an official degree in religious studies. To this

Part 1: Theological Virtues

day, I take one class per semester just for fun! You learn so much in each class that it blends together. However, some of the lessons are embedded in my memory. The following are those that I distinctly remember having that "ahhh" moment where I know and feel the constant love and support of God and how I can continue to foster that relationship.

Through the classes, the primary point of emphasis is the 3 R's: daily prayer with God. *Read*—daily Scripture and/or spiritual reading. *Reflect*—take time to listen to God, in your heart, mind, and soul, regarding what you read. *Resolution*—Based upon your reading and reflection, decide and follow through with whatever it is that God has asked of you. Your resolution has no boundaries. You can make it a short, one day action plan or something you work on daily for a week. The main component is to take action.

I challenge you to find a better place than Eucharistic Adoration to begin your practice of the 3Rs: *Read, Reflect, Resolution*. In your prayerful dialogue with God, He will lead you to the topic and/or Scripture to read and reflect on. I urge you to continue listening to God as He may even nudge you to read about a saint and/or the saint's writings. So, in your Holy Hour you will practice *Read & Reflect*. During your time with God you will be able to decide on your *Resolution*, though you may have to do your *Resolution* outside of the Adoration Chapel. I have held a Holy Hour since I was sixteen years old. I have had many a prayer answered there. I've also laid many a burden on God's shoulders to the point that there is only one set of footprints. About 6 years ago, I was challenged to show up for my Holy Hour empty handed. My teacher said it would be the hardest, yet most beneficial hour of my day. So, I entered the chapel with NOTHING. No books to read. No writing utensils. No journal. My job was to sit in silence and listen for God to speak. My teacher was right. It was sooo tough, yet I felt completely at peace. I continue to practice this method once a month. I mean, how can I say NO to God when He's been so generous, loving, and forgiving towards me? It is my commitment to God (my weekly Holy Hour). Out of respect I show up and listen intensely to what God has to say.

Charity

It is by DAILY practice of the 3R's and frequent visits to Eucharistic Adoration that you will grow closer to God. As you continue with a DAILY Prayer routine that works for your schedule, you will find God front and center ready to help as much as you let Him. The more you rely on God, the attractions of this materialistic world fade. We live in a "me first" society. If it's been invented, I have to have it. If my best friend got a new power tool, I suddenly have to buy an upgraded version of that same tool. If the brand of make-up I wear has 16 lip gloss colors, I will buy ALL colors. I mean, really, what are you going to do with all these products that you "have to" have? As a priest put it when I was eleven years old, there is no plot of ground to park a U-haul on when you die. You can't take it with you. If you can't take it with you when you die, then why exactly is it that you need the products so bad? And need them NOW? That U-haul image is embedded in my brain that even today, I try to avoid the purchases that are more "wants" than "needs". So, yes, it is hard, but not impossible, to dig yourself out of the materialistic pit enveloped around you.

Saint Therese of Liseaux had her faults, but she knew with an absolute truth that the words we speak to one another can either build us up or tear us down. Saint Therese knew about the importance of what Jesus referred to as the two greatest commandments—to love God above all else and to love your neighbor as yourself. It is because Saint Therese recognized and practiced this that she attained sainthood. She knew the power of the spoken word. We, too, witness the power of spoken words. You cannot take your words back. One form of not being able to take your words back is *bullying*.

Similar to the U-haul sermon I heard when I was 11, the "bullying" sermon left a picture embedded in my heart. This sermon was given at an all school Mass. There were 3 simple points to ponder: don't be a bully; don't be a bully helper; and it is okay to tell if someone is being a bully (safety is of the upmost importance). A bully does what it takes to be the center of attention by insulting another person. A bully helper is one who encourages the bully by condoning his or her behavior and getting more people involved.

Part 1: Theological Virtues

Finally, children, especially, tend to tattle on one another. Adults tend to dismiss tattle telling in general. It can become so monotonous that the adults may not even know the topic of what exactly is said. Adults need to emphasize that when someone is in danger or crying that the most important thing they can do is to tell an adult what they saw happen.

Reflection:

Just like in our analogy earlier where we described how kind words can build a person up and unkind words tear them down, we can equate Christians building each other up with love and the bully's tearing their victims apart with use. The opposite of "love" is "use". The bully uses their victim to extract pride for themselves. In this way they "use" their victim. We have no need to dig deeper. Saint Therese of Liseaux is the most fitting example of charity. For it is The Little Flower herself that said, "My vocation, at last I have found it; my vocation is love." When you choose to filter love through your words and actions, everything feels light as a feather. And, at that point you lose all momentum and time to stir up negativity. You are consistently pouring out love.

As stated previously, the opposite of love is not hate. The opposite of love is "use." As an example, let's just say you are bored; all your homework is done and/or you've got all your chores done for the day and/or you're off work and there's nothing to do. So, you dial up your one and only friend and say, "Hey can we hang out?" Now, do you really want to hang out with that person at that time or are you just using that person so that you don't have to face your own boredom?

In contrast to what the world offers, God teaches us to build others up with compassion and love. This is the pulse that keeps us alive. How do we accomplish this? We must obey the two greatest commandments: love God above all others and love your neighbor as yourself. Similar to Saint Therese of Liseaux, we must cultivate a relationship with God with love as the pulse that when pushed hard enough love is outpouring from your very being. But there is

CHARITY

a very important step in between loving God and your neighbor. That step is loving yourself. Ponder this again: love your neighbor as yourself. BINGO. You first must love yourself in a way that self-confidence is gained in order to spread that love to your neighbor. So, right now I ask you to evaluate the love in your heart. Are you choosing to not love your neighbor because you don't love yourself? Or are you choosing to not love your neighbor for another reason? The order of where you place your love does matter. You have to love God first and foremost and then yourself. For it is from your love of God and yourself that others begin to see love in action. But it doesn't end there. Why can't each person in the entire world practice one random act of kindness, not just once, but once per day? When each person practices this daily random act of kindness, it would create a ripple effect, which would be unstoppable. Then, and only then, we would have world peace and harmony.

Question 1: Describe a few ways that you show love in action.

Question 2: What is the big deal about focusing on this concept of love?

Digging Deeper: Argue for or against these Biblical figures exhibiting the virtue of *charity*:

- Damaris upon hearing of Jesus rising from the dead (Acts 17:32-34)

Part 1: Theological Virtues

- The Samaritan Woman at the Well talking with Jesus (John 4:1-26)

- Peter when Jesus asks him to feed His sheep (John 21:15-19)

Prayer: This prayer is a 'primer' to the soul to help your spirit cultivate love first within and then as an intercession to bring together all peoples, all faiths, all religions, or no religion at all, "In a glorious display." A love that is shared and understood by all. This calling is particularly powerful because it joins sinners and saints together to ask for the same forgiveness and the same grace as a result. A whole "city on our knees."

"City On Our Knees"
Tobymac

If you gotta start somewhere why not here
If you gotta start sometime why not now
If we gotta start somewhere I say here
If we gotta start sometime I say now
Through the fog there is hope in the distance
From cathedrals to third world missions
Love will fall to the earth like a crashing wave

Tonight's the night
For the sinners and the saints
Two worlds collide in a beautiful display
It's all love tonight
When we step across the line
We can sail across the sea

Charity

To a city with one king
A city on our knees
A city on our knees
Oh-oh-oh-oh-oh

If you gotta start somewhere why not here
If you gotta start sometime why not now
If we gotta start somewhere I say here
If we gotta start sometime I say now
Through the fog there is hope in the distance
From cathedrals to third world missions
Love will fall to the earth like a crashing wave

Tonight's the night
For the sinners and the saints
Two worlds collide in a beautiful display
It's all love tonight
When we step across the line
We can sail across the sea
To a city with one king
A city on our knees
A city on our knees
Oh-oh-oh

Tonight couldn't last forever
We are one choice from together
Tonight couldn't last forever
Ooh
Tonight couldn't last forever
We are one choice from together
As family
We're family
Oh Tonight couldn't last forever

Part 1: Theological Virtues

We are one choice from together
You and me

Ya, you and me
Tonight's the night
For the sinners and the saints
Two worlds collide
In a glorious display
Cuz its all love tonight

When we step across the line
We can sail across the sea
To a city with one king
A city on our knees
A city on our knees
Oh oh oh
A city on our knees
A city on our knees
Oh oh oh
If we gotta start somewhere why not here
If we gotta start sometime why not now

Part 2

Cardinal Virtues

Prudence

Justice

Fortitude

Temperance

New American Bible Revised Edition

Galatians 5:22-23
"In contrast, the fruit of the Spirit is love, joy, peace, patience, kindness, generosity, faithfulness, gentleness, self-control. Against such there is no law."

Catechism of the Catholic Church

#1834
"The human virtues are stable dispositions of the intellect and the will that govern our acts, order our passions, and guide our conduct in accordance with reason and faith. They can be grouped around the four cardinal virtues: prudence, justice, fortitude, and temperance."

Chapter 4

Prudence

Defined in my own Words: thinking before acting, always with your best intentions of those involved in the situation then choosing the best avenue to fit the situation

Scripture:

> *Proverbs 8:12*
> "I, Wisdom, dwell with prudence, and useful knowledge I have."
>
> *1 Chronicles 22:12*
> "But may the Lord give you prudence and discernment when he gives you command over Israel, so that you keep the law of the Lord, your God."

Catechism of the Catholic Church:

> *#1835*
> "Prudence disposes the practical reason to discern, in every circumstance, our true good and to choose the right means for achieving it."

Sponsored by: Saint Thomas More
Patron Saint of: Adopted Children; Lawyers, Civil Servants, Politicians, Difficult Marriages
Feast Day: June 22
Insight in Saint Thomas More's Words:

PART 2: CARDINAL VIRTUES

"What part soever you take upon you, play that as well as you can and make the best of it."

"Occupy your mind with good thoughts, or the enemy will fill them with bad ones."

Real Lives, Real Stories:

Prudence is one of the four cardinal virtues. The cardinal virtues are different than the theological virtues in that faith, hope, and love are infused in your soul whereas prudence, justice, fortitude, and temperance are graces received and you are responsible for growing in those four virtues. The most prominent aspect of this cardinal virtue of prudence is making decisions based on well-thought-out processes versus instantaneously. In contemplating the best real-life example of prudence, it didn't take too long for me to realize that Pope Francis is the model extraordinaire. As our current pope of the Catholic Church, Pope Francis is a man of firsts. He is the first Jesuit priest to be elevated to pope. He is the first Central American man to hold office. Pope Francis honors his vow of poverty as he chooses to live in a simple apartment with only basic necessities. Instead of being chauffeured, Pope Francis drives an economical car. Though a highly prolific public figure, he is out and about amongst the people, not separated and segregated by them for security reasons. Pope Francis' prayer life is such that he listens to God as to how to handle every situation. The strength of Pope Francis is such that he has a strong internal equilibrium that is capable of overcoming instincts coming from his own character and personal viewpoints. He seeks appropriate counsel for topics ranging from stem cell research to abortion; from peace on earth to illegal immigrants applying for work VISAs; from education to end-of-life issues. Pope Francis lays every decision to be made at the feet of Jesus Christ. He prays about how to deliver the message he wishes to get across to the world. His writings are a reflection of this. Pope Francis looks at the whole picture with a moral compass guiding his thoughts, words, and actions. He is a reflection of the bar that Jesus expects of each of us as Catholic Christians.

Pope Francis describes prudence as the essence of the gift of counsel through the Holy Spirit's guidance that is received upon the sacrament of confirmation. Like Pope Francis, you, too, will learn how to make wise and well thought out decisions based on the knowledge gained in prayer. Let us thank God for Pope Francis' example of prudence that is well noticed by a lot of people throughout the entire world today. For as the Opus Dei leaders have surmised, Pope Francis is a man of God, an example of prudence.

Literally, every decision Pope Francis makes will affect the entire world.

Reflection:

In a nutshell prudence is doing what is good and avoiding evil. In every direction you turn, you can see the evil choices lurking towards you, daring you to follow. This isn't what was intended when God created the world and all that is in it. God's well-formed intention was for all of us humans to enjoy the riches of the world and to bask in His glory and let Him be the Lord and in control of our lives. Then sin entered the world through the evil temptation of the serpent. Eve fell for the temptation, eating the forbidden fruit. She then took it a step further and persuaded Adam to do the same.

This sequence is the essence of the term "concupiscence". "Concupiscence" is the inclination to do what's bad; to do what's against the grain; to go against your religious moral. It is when you follow through with living the way you want without a care in the world as to God's part in the plan. In fact, disregard for God's standard has now become a part of daily human living. To combat this apathetic attitude, God gave us the four cardinal virtues: prudence, justice, fortitude, and temperance. We must study and practice these four virtues almost daily to enable God's graces to flow in us and through us as our ultimate goal is entrance into Heaven.

Part 2: Cardinal Virtues

By just knowing the definition of and relevant examples of "prudence", you are at an advantage to maintain consistent growth in this virtue. There are three components of prudence. The first component of prudence is the information gathering stage. After jotting down all relevant data for a situation, the next step is judgment. It is during the judgment phase that intuition takes over as you may deliberate for quite some time through a myriad of emotions the best solution at this time. The final stage in making a decision is following through with your plan of action. It is highly advised to align your solution with the original problem. Finally, there are times when you only have a split second to make and execute your decision. At these times, just go with your gut instinct. This is kind of like working in emergency type of setting. As you continue to practice, you will become more proficient in making any and all decisions.

The saint that comes to mind as a sponsor to guide us along the path of prudence is St. Thomas More. Saint Thomas discerned the priesthood and deferred to God's answer of "no", you are not called to the priesthood, but rather, married life. Saint Thomas excelled in prudence as well as judgment of character. He continued to advance in his knighthood adventures. He quickly became one of King Henry VIII's greatest workers. Saint Thomas was respectful of King Henry VIII. At the same time, Saint Thomas advocated on the behalf of his religion. Saint Thomas stood in opposition to King Henry VIII divorcing his wife. Saint Thomas never wavered in his alliance to God above all else. These qualities are impressive. Now add to that the fact that Saint Thomas never expressed outward signs of anger towards anyone. That does not imply that Saint Thomas was never angry.

Based on eyewitness testimony of multiple individuals, Saint Thomas was the epitome of "keep calm and pray". Saint Thomas extended mercy to those who needed mercy. The very center of his being was attached to God, and God alone. He focused completely on the task at hand. He did not hang on to the past or worry about the future. Saint Thomas lived in the moment. We should do likewise.

Prudence

Question 1: In what situations do you make spur of the moment decisions? Describe your thought process when you take time to make prudent decisions.

Question 2: Name someone in your life that you turn to in order to think out decisions to be made. How does this person help you organize your thoughts to make the best possible decision for yourself?

Digging Deeper: Argue for or against these Biblical figures exhibiting the virtue of *prudence*:

- David when he plays his harp for Saul (1 Samuel 16:14-23)

- Solomon when planning to build the temple to honor God (2 Chronicles 2:12)

- Deborah when serving as a judge for the Israelites (Judges 4:4-14)

Prayer: Oh God, you are like the ice glistening upon tree branches. Continue to wrap me in Your arms of love lest I bend, even if just ever so slightly, away from Your will. I want to follow in Your way, truth, and life. Amen Jesus.

Chapter 5

Justice

Defined in my own Words: awareness of a particular situation with the ability to see each person's point of view, thus being fair to all involved.

Scripture:

> *Isaiah 30:18*
> "Therefore the Lord waits to be gracious to you; therefore he will rise up to show mercy to you. For the Lord is a God of justice; blessed are all those who wait for him."

> *Luke 18:7*
> "And will not God grant justice to his chosen ones who cry to him day and night? Will he delay long in helping them?"

> *Galatians 3:11*
> "And that no one is justified before God by the law is clear, for "the one who is righteous by faith will live." "

Catechism of the Catholic Church:

> *#1040*
> "The Last Judgment will come when Christ returns in glory. Only the Father knows the day and the hour; only he determines the moment of its coming. Then through his Son Jesus Christ he will pronounce the final word on

JUSTICE

all history. We shall know the ultimate meaning of the whole work of creation and of the entire economy of salvation and understand the marvellous ways by which his Providence led everything towards its final end. The Last Judgment will reveal that God's justice triumphs over all the injustices committed by his creatures and that God's love is stronger than death." [628]

[628] Cf. Song 8:6.

#1807
"Justice is the moral virtue that consists in the constant and firm will to give their due to God and neighbor. Justice toward God is called the "virtue of religion." Justice toward men disposes one to respect the rights of each and to establish in human relationships the harmony that promotes equity with regard to persons and to the common good. The just man, often mentioned in the Sacred Scriptures, is distinguished by habitual right thinking and the uprightness of his conduct toward his neighbor. "You shall not be partial to the poor or defer to the great, but in righteousness shall you judge your neighbor." [68] "Masters, treat your slaves justly and fairly, knowing that you also have a Master in heaven." "[69]

[68] Lev 19:15.
[69] Col 4:1.

#1836
"Justice consists in the firm and constant will to give God and neighbor their due."

Sponsored by: Saint Thomas Aquinas
Patron Saint of: all Catholic educational establishments
Feast Day: January 28
Insight in Saint Thomas Aquinas' Words:

> "He who is not angry when there is just cause for anger is immoral. Why? Because anger looks to the good of justice. And if you can live amid injustice without anger, you are immoral as well as unjust."

Part 2: Cardinal Virtues

"Justice is a certain rectitude of mind whereby a man does what he ought to do in the circumstances confronting him."

"Mercy without justice is the mother of dissolution; justice without mercy is cruelty."

Real Lives, Real Stories:

"I pledge allegiance to the flag of the United States of America and to the republic for which it stands one nation under God indivisible with liberty and justice for all". (Pledge of Allegiance)

"Neither slavery nor involuntary servitude, except as a punishment for crime whereof the party shall have been duly convicted, shall exist within the United States, or any place subject to their jurisdiction." (13th Amendment to the Constitution of the United States of America)

I vividly recall reciting the "Pledge of Allegiance" daily as young as Kindergarten. At that age, I didn't realize the power of the words and that the essence of the pledge was our way of expressing thanks for the freedom(s) it represents. Fast forward to my first job after college graduation: a Kindergarten teacher. Part of our daily morning routine, just after the day began, was reciting the "Pledge of Allegiance". Everyone stood still placing his/her right hand on his/her heart. In all of my years of teaching Kindergarten, not one person in my presence veered from "the rules".

In contrast, as an elementary school student, I recall learning that President Abraham Lincoln was responsible for freeing the slaves. Looking back, I cannot remember the specific details I learned. I do not remember learning the 13th Amendment to the Constitution of the United States of America.

Now, let's take a look at President Lincoln's failures, successes, campaign elements, and the issue of slavery. During President-elect Abraham Lincoln's campaign back in 1860, the pinnacle was the topic of slavery. I wonder if Lincoln realized how important his position of slavery was and the vitality of abolishing slavery at any level. Any change to the current issues of slavery would be successful. That was Lincoln's primary selling point. And after successfully campaigning, President Lincoln began implementing the changes he promised the country.

I'm not so sure that President Lincoln knew exactly how important, vital, and reminiscent of our country today as we see it is. Appendix A shows the failures and successes of Abraham Lincoln from a young, aspiring politician to the pinnacle of his presidency with the signing of the Emancipation Proclamation and the ratification of the 13th Amendment to the Constitution of the United States of America. Appendix B is the text of The Emancipation Proclamation. These two documents declared the slaves free. At the time of these two documents there were "slave states" and "free states". It was in the "slave states" where slaves were set free. Finally, justice for all.

Reflection:

As we continue deeper into this reflection of justice, hopefully you have seen a pattern over the first four chapters and recognize the importance of growing and learning in virtue each day. As we live a virtuous life, we are given the grace of God to respond to God. That's what it takes to be happy. Virtues are skills that we must develop. . .as we succeed in the virtues, we become happy. God is the sole just judge that in the end will decide where you spend eternity. What can you do now to ensure that you will spend eternity in Heaven with God? The single most important action you can control is to love God fully and totally; placing Him first in your life. Daily. That is a tall order. It is definitely do-able; with gobs of hard work. You may not feel successful each day. That's okay. You are giving 100% effort. We looked at President Lincoln's failures and successes. I think it's time to evaluate your successes to learn and grow in God. Your job is to listen and discern God's will for your life and to act on that will that God has prepared for you. God sees through our deepest soul to our true colors. Will you turn to Jesus and let Him reign completely in your life or will you tug and pull against His will, continuing in a spiral of making your own decisions? One way to look at your relationship with Jesus is to use the acronym JOY.

God modeled justice to show us the way of LOVE. Justice shows me that if I'm living gratitude, a life of love, I must place others first. If I only thought of self, I would feel entitled to anything and everything. This is serious backwards thinking...I owe others. Think of this acronym:

Jesus Others You

I OWE God. God has created me freely out of LOVE. I must think of God first. I am to give generously my time, talent, and treasure.

Now, consider God's role in the virtue of justice. Justice is a skill at doing something right. It is basically giving to others what I owe them. So, why do we owe anyone anything anyways? It is because we are called to LOVE, out of LOVE for God. In essence, we pay it forward. We don't withhold anything that belongs to another. We are especially called to recognize the gift of life. The gift of life is tied to LOVE and gratitude. We owe others dignity of the human person. Justice promotes three different kinds of relationships: relationship with God; relationships with individuals; and relationships with societies.

The two greatest commandments are: love God with your whole heart and love your neighbor as yourself. It flows then, that if you have an understanding about what you owe God, it is time to consider what you owe your neighbor. Justice towards your neighbor is impossible without God. Your neighbor has these rights: to their life; to a good name, reputation; to be respected; to the truth; etc. The ultimate example of justice is the Bible story of The Good Samaritan (Luke 10:30-37). When we strive to reach that level of goodwill towards our neighbor, God will look down upon us with a smile. If you are truly practicing the two greatest commandments, then you will have your head on your shoulders expressing justice towards societies. The most basic of all societies is the family. It is in the family setting that virtues are cultivated. The role of children in families is to give their parents gratitude, respect, and deference through obedience. The role of mothers in families is to take care

JUSTICE

of the family by being a homemaker and raising the children. The role of fathers is to be present to the family and make time for the family. Fathers do need to work, but their work should never be at the abandonment of the family.

Finally, let's look at the life of Saint Thomas Aquinas and how he excelled in the virtue of justice. Saint Thomas Aquinas, a doctor of the Catholic Church, has quite a bit to say about justice for all. Saint Thomas Aquinas was a just judge. Saint Thomas Aquinas proclaimed that the government should be separate from offering justice to those who need it most. For example, we all have personal belongings in our homes where we reside. It is our job, with God's grace, to decide what to do with our belongings. No government input is needed. The steps we need to take to better ourselves for entrance to the kingdom of God, Heaven, does not need government intervention. Saint Thomas Aquinas' goal as a doctor of the church was to make that known to all.

The key to right relationships with God, individuals, and societies is forgiveness. Yeah, I know, there are so many reasons why we refuse to forgive: hurts too bad; attachment to offense; lack of experience; pride; fear, etc. You must let go of all these excuses and turn towards the path of forgiveness. Justice is giving what is due. Mercy is going beyond what is due. Have your mind, heart, and soul focused on mercy and God will meet your every need.

Question 1: Which Bible passage, Catechism number, and Saint Thomas Aquinas quote (from above) depicts what is near and dear to your heart? Explain.

Part 2: Cardinal Virtues

Question 2: What is one beam in my eye that I need to rid myself of before I try to take the speck out of another's eye? How will I accomplish this?

Digging Deeper: Argue for or against these Biblical figures exhibiting the virtue of *justice*:

- Pontius Pilate when Jesus was brought before him (John 18:28-38)

- Lazarus being raised from the dead (John 11:1-44)

- The Adulteress Woman who was NOT stoned to death (John 8:1-11)

Prayer: Dear Lord Jesus, There are so many "unjust" acts we witness as humans. Please help me focus on myself by offering up my own unjust acts. Please teach me how to help those around me in need. Please let your grace flow freely through me so that I may be an example to those in need, while not judging them. I thank you for being an example of justice. Amen Jesus.

Chapter 6

Fortitude

Defined in my own Words: Courage; Bravery; doing what is right amidst pressure to do wrong; and when life is threatened, the ability to endure acts of violence and what is necessary to repair the damage done by acts of violence.

Scripture:

> *Deuteronomy 31:6*
> "Be strong and steadfast; have no fear or dread of them, for it is the LORD, your God, who marches with you; he will never fail you or forsake you."

Catechism of the Catholic Church:

> *#1837*
> "Fortitude ensures firmness in difficulties and constancy in the pursuit of the good."

Sponsored by: Saint Bakhita
Patron Saint of: the victims of slavery and trafficked persons
Feast Day: February 8
Insight in Saint Bakhita's Words:

> "If I were to meet the slave-traders who kidnapped me and even those who tortured me, I would kneel and kiss their hands, for if that did not happen, I would not be a Christian and Religious today. . . The Lord has loved

me so much: we must love everyone... we must be compassionate!"

Real Lives, Real Stories:

Courageousness and bravery, especially before, during, and after acts of violence, are synonyms of fortitude. Two words and internet access will send you to a myriad of articles on the two-word topic: Wichita Massacre. It is in these gruesome, descriptive articles that you will become familiar with the lone survivor (known only as H.G. out of respect for her healing) of the Wichita Massacre (December 2000). H.G. testified the bloody truth that sent the Carr brothers to prison and on death row. For three hours that night, H.G. and four friends were raped, sodomized, tortured, blackmailed, burglarized, and shot in the head. Not only did H.G. exhibit fortitude during the acts of violence, in the aftermath of that night, she did everything right. That night, I lost two amazing friends and prayer warriors. There is no doubt that Saint Bakhita was praying from Heaven as these five individuals were abused. Why? Saint Bakhita was eight when she was kidnapped in a slave raid and forced into many things by four different slave masters. And I have no doubt in my mind that all five of the Wichita Massacre victims went down praying for their murderers similar to how Jesus did on the cross that Good Friday afternoon. Had it not been for H.G.'s hair clip, in my opinion, the remorseless Carr brothers would have continued their killing spree.

The irony of this vicious act of violence is that while the Carr brothers remain stone cold after all these years, Heather's mother stood at the podium on the altar during her daughter's funeral and in what can only be described as a state of grace, in front of 1000+ people, publicly forgave the Carr brothers. This act of bravery is another piece of Christianity in action and a prime example of fortitude.

Reflection:

Fortitude is expressed in many forms. Some examples are: the 9/11 terrorist attack on America, including all who lost their lives and the many who stepped forward to defend their country; Captain Sully landing the plane on the Hudson River where all on board the escaped; Hurricane Katrina victims and those offering their very lives to save another, practically strangers; and many football players speaking about chronic traumatic encephalopathy (CTE) to the point of making wills to donate their brains for research upon their deaths.

Above are some of the many examples my teacher in the faith taught me during a two-semester course on the virtues. In addition to the many real-life examples of each virtue, my teacher has exposed me to many other saints. Some of the saints he shares about are very well known. Others are obscure. Without my teacher's enthusiasm, I would be reserved to the point that I would not research on my own.

That is how I was introduced to Saint Josephine Bakhita. Saint Bakhita grew up with five siblings. She experienced a joyful, carefree life until the age of eight. At the age of eight, amidst her typical Sudanese environment, Saint Bakhita was kidnapped by Arab slave traders. Arab slave traders came through the area regularly and kidnapped children to be their slaves. Saint Bakhita remained in slavery for 12 years. During those 12 years she was traded four different times. All four of those slave owners drove her way past the limits of every kind of emotional scar and physical scar that you can imagine. Saint Bakhita was so scarred by her experience as a slave that she could no longer remember her birth name. She began going by the name Bakhita, which means "fortunate one".

It was when Saint Bakhita was a slave under these four owners that she endured physical and emotional torture, yet never once complained. It was the fifth slave owner of Saint Bakhita that treated her otherwise.

This fifth slave owner treated Saint Bakhita as a human being with dignity, not as a slave. This slave owner NEVER beat Saint

Part 2: Cardinal Virtues

Bakhita. He NEVER did anything to harm her. It was this slave owner who taught Saint Bakhita about God. Until this time, Saint Bakhita knew about God, but didn't know God as three persons in one or that Jesus died for us to save us from Hell.

It was during this time of the 5th slave owner that Saint Bakhita realized she was free in Christ. She continued to give God the glory. It was also around this time that she was declared FREE from slavery.

Eventually, this fifth slave owner needed to relocate to Italy, Saint Bakhita begged that owner to take her with him. He did. There was a time when that slave trader needed to go out of town, he placed Saint Bakhita under the care of the Canossian Sisters in Venice, Italy. It was when Saint Bakhita was under the care of these sisters that she felt called to follow Christ. She entered that community and ministered 42 years.

So, yes, we do have modern day examples of fortitude, but one would be remiss to not study and recognize the power of God that lived in saints from the past like Saint Bakhita.

Question 1: What is the process you use to remain steadfast in the Lord?

Question 2: How would you respond to a family member or friend if he/she confided to you that he/she was a victim of acts of violence?

Fortitude

Digging Deeper: Argue for or against these Biblical figures exhibiting the virtue of *fortitude*:

- Abraham as he offered his son Isaac as a sacrifice (Genesis 22:1-19)

- Moses as he led God's people through the Red Sea (Exodus 14: 19-31)

- Daniel in the lion's den (Daniel 6:1-28)

Prayer: Dear Lord Jesus, you are the ultimate example of fortitude, for you withstood terrible acts of violence during your ministry, especially before and during your death on the cross. Please gently prod me when I fail to recognize that if you could endure all that you did, so too, can I. Use me. Guide me that by my actions, others will see that You are the source of my courage to stand beside you, pointing upward, giving You all the glory. Amen Jesus.

Chapter 7

Temperance

Defined in my own Words: self-control; placing limits on your actions; knowing when to stop and say "NO"
Scripture:

> *2 Peter 1: 3;5-8*
> "His divine power has bestowed on us everything that makes for life and devotion, through the knowledge of him who called us by his own glory and power.[d] [e]For this very reason, make every effort to supplement your faith with virtue, virtue with knowledge, knowledge with self-control, self-control with endurance, endurance with devotion, devotion with mutual affection, mutual affection with love. If these are yours and increase in abundance, they will keep you from being idle or unfruitful in the knowledge of our Lord Jesus Christ."

Catechism of the Catholic Church:

> *#1838*
> "Temperance moderates the attraction of the pleasures of the senses and provides balance in the use of created goods."

Sponsored by: Saint Francis of Assisi
Patron Saint of: Animals
Feast Day: October 4

TEMPERANCE

Insight in Saint Francis of Assisi's Words:

> "Remember that when you leave this earth, you can take with you nothing that you have received -only what you have given: a full heart, enriched by honest service, love, sacrifice and courage."

> "Start by doing what's necessary; then do what's possible; and suddenly you are doing the impossible."

> "Preach the Gospel at all times and when necessary use words."

Real Lives, Real Stories:

I'm not sure who talked the most in their married life: Uncle Kenneth or Aunt Edna. They both talked ALL the time. In fact, there were times their voices escalated because each was trying to vie for attention from the other. And most definitely each wanted their thoughts heard, trying to bask in the glory of their view. At the same time, they had a rock-solid marriage and loved each other more than anyone except God. It is in remembrance of those gone before me that I can ponder their point of view and which virtue would the memory be an example of. In this case, the virtue I see is temperance. Well, actually, it's what temperance does not look like. Saint Francis of Assisi said it best when he spoke, "Preach the Gospel at all times and when necessary use words." You see, the most important quality in Uncle Kenneth and Aunt Edna was their love for one another. They focused on getting each other to Heaven. I do have memories where Uncle Kenneth talked more than Aunt Edna and vice versa. I am by no means judging either one of them. In fact, I'm smiling now because of the loving memory of their dedication to one another; chatting their days away.

    Saint Francis of Assisi was another living example of temperance. You hear of "rags to riches" stories nearly every day. Saint Francis was unique in that era where poverty was visible, his childhood was quite the opposite. He was born into wealth and had everything he wanted at his disposal. Yet, it was in the quiet of his

Part 2: Cardinal Virtues

heart that he heard Jesus calling. Saint Francis left everything he had to follow Jesus. He lived with the bare minimum to exist in that era.

In my lifespan, I have heard many a sermon. I have generated a Top 10 list of the best sermons I have heard in person. Near the top was a sermon about material possessions. The priest spoke about what it is that draws us to buy more, more, and even more. We see it. We have to have it. This happens frequently. The point that hit me hard was when the priest said when we die we can't take anything with us. There's no space for a U-Haul next to your body in the cemetery. You don't need it in Heaven. So why do you need it now? To this day I can picture a U-Haul next to a grave and shake my head at that silly notion.

In the Roman Catholic Church, millions of people change their lifestyle for the 40 days before Easter. We practice prayer, fasting, and almsgiving each Lent. Look through this abbreviated list of what you can fast from and you will see temperance at work:

- Shopping Online
- Speaking
- Sugar
- Video Games
- TV Shows
- Eating Out
- Soda
- Music

Now take another good, hard look at the ideas for temperance above. How can you make your next Lenten experience deeper and richer than before? Not only that, but you must ask yourself if your fasting experience ends on Easter Sunday or will it continue past the 40 days of Lent. I mean, what is the point of Lent to suffer without for 40 days and then pick up the old habits the second the clock hits 12AM Easter Sunday? Why not extend your fasting indefinitely, especially if you are a better person because of it?

Temperance

Reflection:

We live in a "me first" society. From the time we are born, society pushes and pulls us to strive for more, more, and even more. The technical term for this is "concupiscence". "Concupiscence" has hold of us the minute we are born. It is the basic human desire for things that we know aren't good for us. This human desire drives us into obtaining more things than we know what to do with. Are you purchasing more to compete with a friend? Are you eating a second helping because it's there? Are you a perfectionist, arriving so early to an event so you can be served first? Are you purchasing items online out of boredom or spite? Do you underbudget just so you can have extra online shopping because you want mail? Do you upgrade to the highest price level with all purchases to get the best of the best? Are you the first to volunteer for every activity that comes your way? Do you have an invisible wall around your body to separate yourself indicating that it's all about you? These are examples of the ways that concupiscence has infiltrated our society. So, what is the remedy for this?

The remedy to counteract this basic human desire is to practice living countercultural to what the world has to offer. Living countercultural means actively saying "NO" to things that come your way. The cornerstone to living countercultural to what the world offers lies within your power: the power to say "NO". The more you say "NO", the easier it becomes to withstand peer pressure. That is the essence of temperance: self-control; the ability to say "NO" when the world screams "YES".

For my family, a significant, stable, resource for us is our church family. Knowing we have an invaluable church family reminds us to not only think before we act, but also think before we speak. Our church has a few permanent Bible study groups. We are the leaders for one group. It is in weekly Bible Study discussion that we share our successes and ways to do better. We spend time processing the terms defined above (concupiscence & countercultural) and dream of a society that bases life upon those words. We talk about daily prayer centered on the three R's: Read (God's

Part 2: Cardinal Virtues

Word or Spiritual reading or both), Reflect (on what was read), and Resolution (practicing what touched your heart). We hold each other accountable for daily prayer. We inquire when one is absent from daily Mass. We pray for those who miss Bible study every now and then because of one thing or another. We lift each other up rather than tear one another down. We share the tools needed to practice temperance in the here and now. And the finest tool of all is called prayer.

Question 1: What are the most convenient ways to practice temperance? How can you challenge yourself to go deeper; practicing temperance in a way that is uncomfortable at first, but leads to a better you?

Question 2: How can you incorporate Read, Reflect, and Resolution into your daily routine? Who can you ask to hold you accountable for practicing your resolution?

Digging Deeper: Argue for or against these Biblical figures exhibiting the virtue of *temperance*:

- Samson being pursued by Delilah (Judges 16:4-22)

Temperance

- Joseph being sold into slavery (Genesis 37:12-28)

- Jesus being tempted in the desert (Matthew 4:1-11)

Prayer: Let us conclude this virtue of temperance with The Peace Prayer, or better known as The Prayer of Saint Francis: "Lord, make me an instrument of Your peace. Where there is hatred, let me sow love; where there is injury, pardon; where there is doubt, faith; where there is despair, hope; where there is darkness, light; where there is sadness, joy. O, Divine Master, grant that I may not so much seek to be consoled as to console; to be understood as to understand; to be loved as to love; For it is in giving that we receive; it is in pardoning that we are pardoned; it is in dying that we are born again to eternal life."

Part 3

Human Virtues Close to My Heart
Patience

Compassion

Perseverance

Authenticity

Purposefulness

New American Bible Revised Edition

Philippians 4:4-8
"Rejoice[a] in the Lord always. I shall say it again: rejoice! Your kindness[b] should be known to all. The Lord is near. Have no anxiety at all, but in everything, by prayer and petition, with thanksgiving, make your requests known to God. Then the peace of God that surpasses all understanding will guard your hearts and minds in Christ Jesus. Finally, brothers, whatever is true, whatever is honorable, whatever is just, whatever is pure, whatever is lovely, whatever is gracious, if there is any excellence and if there is anything worthy of praise, think about these things.[c]"

Catechism of the Catholic Church

#1804
"*Human virtues* are firm attitudes, stable dispositions, habitual perfections of intellect and will that govern our

actions, order our passions, and guide our conduct according to reason and faith. They make possible ease, self-mastery, and joy in leading a morally good life. The virtuous man is he who freely practices the good.

The moral virtues are acquired by human effort. They are the fruit and seed of morally good acts; they dispose all the powers of the human being for communion with divine love."

Chapter 8

Patience

Defined in my own Words: calm demeanor that surpasses any friction
Scripture:

> *Romans 15:1-6*
> "We who are strong ought to put up with the failings of the weak and not to please ourselves; let each of us please our neighbor for the good, for building up. For Christ did not please himself; but, as it is written, "The insults of those who insult you fall upon me."[a] For whatever was written previously was written for our instruction, that by endurance and by the encouragement of the scriptures we might have hope. May the God of endurance and encouragement grant you to think in harmony[b] with one another, in keeping with Christ Jesus, that with one accord you may with one voice glorify the God and Father of our Lord Jesus Christ."

15:3 Liberation from the law of Moses does not make the scriptures of the old covenant irrelevant. Much consolation and motivation for Christian living can be derived from the Old Testament, as in the citation from Ps 69:10. Because this psalm is quoted several times in the New Testament, it has been called indirectly messianic.

Part 3: Human Virtues Close to My Heart

15:5 Think in harmony: a Greco-Roman ideal. Not rigid uniformity of thought and expression but thoughtful consideration of other people's views finds expression here.

> *Galatians 5:19-23*
> "[a]Now the works of the flesh are obvious: immorality, impurity, licentiousness, idolatry, sorcery, hatreds, rivalry, jealousy, outbursts of fury, acts of selfishness, dissensions, factions, occasions of envy,[b] drinking bouts, orgies, and the like. I warn you, as I warned you before, that those who do such things will not inherit the kingdom of God.
> In contrast, the fruit of the Spirit is love, joy, peace, patience, kindness, generosity, faithfulness, gentleness, self-control. Against such there is no law."

5:19-23 Such lists of vices and virtues (cf. Rom 1:29-31; 1 Cor 6:9-10) were common in the ancient world. Paul contrasts works of the flesh (Gal 5:19) with fruit (not "works") of the Spirit (Gal 5:22). Not law, but the Spirit, leads to such traits.

5:21 Occasions of envy: after the Greek word *phthonoi*, "envies," some manuscripts add a similar sounding one, *phonoi*, "murders."

> *James 5:10*
> "Take as an example of hardship and patience, brothers, the prophets who spoke in the name of the Lord."

Catechism of the Catholic Church:

> *#2613*
> "Three principal *parables* on prayer are transmitted to us by St. Luke:
> The first, "the importunate friend," [75] invites us to urgent prayer: "Knock, and it will be opened to you." To the one who prays like this, the heavenly Father will "give whatever he needs," and above all the Holy Spirit who contains all gifts.
> The second, "the importunate widow," [76] is centered on one of the qualities of prayer: it is necessary to pray always without ceasing and with the *patience* of faith.

"And yet, when the Son of Man comes, will he find faith on earth?"

The third parable, "the Pharisee and the tax collector," [77] concerns the *humility* of the heart that prays. "God, be merciful to me a sinner!" The Church continues to make this prayer its own: Kyrie eleison!"

[75] Cf. Lk 11:5-13.
[76] Cf. Lk 18:1-8.
[77] Cf. Lk 18:9-14.

Sponsored by: Saint Elizabeth of Hungary
Patron Saint of: bakers, beggars, brides, charities, death of children
Feast Day: November 17
Insight in Saint Elizabeth of Hungary's Words:

"As in Heaven Your will is punctually performed, so may it be done on earth by all creatures, particularly in me and by me."

"How could I bear a crown of gold when the Lord bears a crown of thorns? And bears it for me!"

"We are made loveless by our possessions."

Real Lives, Real Stories:

It is out of the mouths of babes that some of the most profound wisdom is spoken and as a result, pondered. A few years ago, a young child in our parish (age four at the time) dressed up for the annual All Saints Day parade at our parish. When asked which saint she was depicting, she confidently replied, "I'm Elizabeth and I'm hungry." That's when my mind connected with that play on words to describe hunger for God. And it is when that deep hunger for God is attained that you begin to feel peace. God patiently awaited for you to return to Him. You could be that next person patiently guiding another person in the faith.

Sunday Mass is an obligation in the Catholic Church. Being completely honest with yourself, do you crave God's love in action being poured out during Sunday Mass? Or do you go to

Part 3: Human Virtues Close to My Heart

Mass solely because it is required? After Mass, do you feel God's outpouring love lived out in Jesus Christ? Let's take it a step further. Does Sunday Mass propel you to share God's love for all? Or do you retreat to your daily routine only to repeat the following weekend? Perhaps God nudges you to go a step further and you feel called to be more than a Sunday Mass attendee. There are so many ministries within your parish to choose from. The key is to want to WANT TO become a more active member in your parish.

When, at long last, you decide to be more active in your parish, God will lead you to the area in which you can best use your time, talent, and treasure. The key is to be open and honest with God and in His time, He will provide opportunities for you. That is what I admire most about my mom. She is very active in her parish. She never misses Sunday Mass and Holy Days of Obligation. She shows up for her weekly Holy Hour. She provides food for funeral luncheons and attends funerals of those she admires most. But the best part of my mom's ministry is that more than any of the above added together, she patiently visits the sick and dying several times a week. My mom visited one friend daily for three months before that friend died. She took care of her mother-in-law for roughly five years. There are many more family members and friends I could name that my mom extended her patient, loving hands to as she took care of them. Mom always knows the right things to say in any given moment. She knows when to sit quietly letting her actions speak louder than words she doesn't utter.

All of this is going on and my mom was not even Catholic. My mom was born and raised in the Methodist faith. She and my daddy got married in the Catholic church and she fulfilled her words as she helped my daddy raise me and my only sibling in the Catholic faith. My job was to NOT try and recruit her to the Catholic faith. I knew God had that covered. I do recall a couple times I asked my mom questions about her faith and the Catholic church. She replied that she could find God anywhere. Since I didn't pester my mom about becoming Catholic, I was completely thrown for a loop when I was told by my daddy that mom was indeed becoming Catholic. My parents attended RCIA classes for 10 months. Mom entered the Catholic Church at Easter 2017. I still get that surreal feeling when I go to communion with MY mom! In my adolescent years, I began having severe panic attacks. My mom was always there for me. She was the solid, patient rock calming me down with each attack. I can still hear her saying, "Holly, breathe. Everything is going to be fine. Take more deep breaths. You will make it." My mom stayed by my side during every panic attack. She also made several doctor appointments for me and took me to every appointment. My mom sat patiently in each waiting room and helped me to stay calm. She patiently listened to each doctor as he/she responded to every question my mom asked. When the cause of my panic attacks was revealed, my mom patiently studied about the medication I was prescribed. She gently made sure I took the medication as prescribed. She made follow-up doctor appointments for me and took me to every appointment. It is because of my mom's patient, calm demeanor that I am where I am today.

I must also offer one last example of my mother's patient demeanor. My parents have been married over 50 years now. Yes, I said 50 YEARS. Marriage has its trials and successes as well as failures and triumphs. It takes a lot of patience to stay married that long. I have witnessed my mom living her marriage vows patiently as far back as I remember.

Reflection:

Saint Elizabeth of Hungary was born into a family of nobility. From an early age, she had an undeniable hunger for Jesus Christ, Our Lord. Saint Elizabeth didn't just talk the talk, she actually walked the walk. She began caring for the sick and destitute from this early age until her death at the young age of 24. At fourteen years of age, Saint Elizabeth married. Her husband always supported Saint Elizabeth's patient service to the sick and destitute. Being of nobility, Saint Elizabeth was able to take everything she owned and with every fiber of her being cared for the sick and the destitute. Saint Elizabeth would insist on giving the clothes off of

PART 3: HUMAN VIRTUES CLOSE TO MY HEART

her very back to the naked. She would go hungry for one or two days just to feed those in need. It was during the hands-on caring that Saint Elizabeth noticed a need for hospitals. As a response to this observation, Saint Elizabeth opened a hospital. Every one of the 28 beds were immediately occupied. She continued hands-on caring for all occupants.

Amidst all of these charitable works, Saint Elizabeth experienced a tragedy. While pregnant with her third child, Saint Elizabeth's husband died. Her response to her husband's death was spending even more time with God and continuing to patiently care for the sick and destitute.

It was at this time that Saint Elizabeth began to seek spiritual direction from the Franciscans. It was through her association of the Franciscans that she heard God's call. Saint Elizabeth set herself apart from the "real world" and joined the Third Order of Saint Francis.

As I picture Saint Elizabeth of Hungary hungry for the Word of God; hungry for all that God has in store for her, I cannot help but picture in my mind the song *"Take Me In"*. I also hear *"Take Me In"* in my mind when I think about my mom's newfound hunger for God after ten months of lessons and becoming "officially" Catholic. Saint Elizabeth and my mom have one thing in common: both love Jesus more than anyone in the whole entire world. Both will do anything to find Jesus at any given moment.

Jesus is at the heart of all that matters. The more you strive to let Jesus take you into his holy of holies, into where he shed his blood for you, the closer you feel to Jesus. When your hunger for God's loveliness consumes every fiber of your being, you are standing in the holy of holies.

I ask you to keep this in mind when thinking about the virtue of patience: what is your reason for asking God for patience? Once you answer that question honestly with your whole heart, deep in the depths of your heart, how can you not see God's patient love for you waiting for you to say, "take me in, Lord."

Patience

"Take Me In"

Take me past the outer courts Into the Holy Place
Past the brazen altar
Lord I want to see your face
Pass me by the crowds of people
And the Priests who sing your praise
I hunger and thirst for your righteousness
But it's only found in one place

[Chorus:]
Take me into the holy of holies
Take me in by the blood of the lamb
Take me into the holy of holies
Take the coal, touch my lips, here I am

Question 1: What images come to your mind when you reflect deeply on the words to the song *"Take Me In"*?

Question 2: Name one person that you find yourself being impatient with on a regular basis. Name one concrete example how you can begin to have more patience with that person.

PART 3: HUMAN VIRTUES CLOSE TO MY HEART

Digging Deeper: Argue for or against these Biblical figures exhibiting the virtue of *patience*:

- Samuel hearing the Lord in the night (3:1-21)

- Joseph upon hearing he was to take Mary, with child, as his wife and raise Jesus as his own (Matthew 1:18-25)

- Uriah when David asked him to go to battle (2 Samuel 11:1-27)

Prayer: Dear Lord Jesus, daily you await patiently for me to come to you in praise and/or in time of need. Please teach me how to patiently await all that You have in store for me as You unfold Your plans for me in Your timing; NOT mine. Amen Jesus.

Chapter 9

Compassion

Defined in my own Words: sincere interest in another's suffering and being willing to help overcome the suffering
Scripture:

> *Micah 7:18-20*
> "[a]Who is a God like you, who removes guilt and pardons sin for the remnant of his inheritance; Who does not persist in anger forever, but instead delights in mercy,
>
> And will again have compassion on us, treading underfoot our iniquities? You will cast into the depths of the sea all our sins;
>
> You will show faithfulness to Jacob, and loyalty to Abraham, As you have sworn to our ancestors from days of old."

a 7:18-20 The final lines of the book contain a hymn of praise for the incomparable God, who pardons sin and delights in mercy. Thus the remnant, those left after the exile, is confident in God's compassion and in the ancient promises sworn to the ancestors.

> *2 Corinthians 1:3-4*
> "Blessed be the God and Father of our Lord Jesus Christ, the Father of compassion and God of all encouragement,[a] who encourages us in our every affliction, so that we may be able to encourage those who

Part 3: Human Virtues Close to My Heart

are in any affliction with the encouragement with which we ourselves are encouraged by God."

a 1:3 **God of all encouragement:** Paul expands a standard Jewish blessing so as to state the theme of the paragraph. The theme of "encouragement" or "consolation" (*paraklēsis*) occurs ten times in this opening, against a background formed by multiple references to "affliction" and "suffering."

> *Peter 3:8-9*
> "Finally, all of you, be of one mind, sympathetic, loving toward one another, compassionate, humble. Do not return evil for evil, or insult for insult; but, on the contrary, a blessing, because to this you were called, that you might inherit a blessing."

Catechism of the Catholic Church:

> *#1503*
> "Christ's compassion toward the sick and his many healings of every kind of infirmity are a resplendent sign that "God has visited his people" [104] and that the Kingdom of God is close at hand. Jesus has the power not only to heal, but also to forgive sins; [105] he has come to heal the whole man, soul and body; he is the physician the sick have need of. [106] His compassion toward all who suffer goes so far that he identifies himself with them: "I was sick and you visited me." [107] His preferential love for the sick has not ceased through the centuries to draw the very special attention of Christians toward all those who suffer in body and soul. It is the source of tireless efforts to comfort them."

[104] Lk 7:16; cf. Mt 4:24.
[105] Cf. Mk 2:5-12.
[106] Cf. Mk 2:17
[107] Mt 25:36.

> *#2843*
> "Thus the Lord's words on forgiveness, the love that loves to the end, [142] become a living reality. The parable of the merciless servant, which crowns the Lord's teaching on

ecclesial communion, ends with these words: "So also my heavenly Father will do to every one of you, if you do not forgive your brother from your heart." [143] It is there, in fact, "in the depths of the *heart*," that everything is bound and loosed. It is not in our power not to feel or to forget an offense; but the heart that offers itself to the Holy Spirit turns injury into compassion and purifies the memory in transforming the hurt into intercession."

[42] Cf. Jn 13:1.
[143] Cf. Mt 18:23-35.

Sponsored by: Saint Joseph
Patron Saint of: the universal church, fathers, families
Feast Day: March 19
Insight in Saint Joseph's Words:

"Clearly, what God wants above all is our will which we received as a free gift from God in creation and possess as though our own. When a man trains himself to acts of virtue, it is with the help of grace from God from whom all good things come that he does this. The will is what man has as his unique possession."

"We are born to love, we live to love, and we will die to love still more."

Real Lives, Real Stories:

One needs to look no further than The Bible itself for a prime example of compassion. Let's review the story of Joseph, the carpenter, the foster father of Jesus.

Matthew 1:18-25
"Now this is how the birth of Jesus Christ came about. When his mother Mary was betrothed to Joseph,[a] but before they lived together, she was found with child through the holy Spirit. Joseph her husband, since he was a righteous man,[b] yet unwilling to expose her to shame, decided to divorce her quietly. Such was his intention when, behold, the angel of the Lord[c] appeared

Part 3: Human Virtues Close to My Heart

> to him in a dream and said, "Joseph, son of David, do not be afraid to take Mary your wife into your home. For it is through the holy Spirit that this child has been conceived in her. She will bear a son and you are to name him Jesus,[d] because he will save his people from their sins." All this took place to fulfill what the Lord had said through the prophet: [e]"Behold, the virgin shall be with child and bear a son, and they shall name him Emmanuel," which means "God is with us." When Joseph awoke, he did as the angel of the Lord had commanded him and took his wife into his home. He had no relations with her until she bore a son,[f] and he named him Jesus."

1:18 Betrothed to Joseph: betrothal was the first part of the marriage, constituting a man and woman as husband and wife. Subsequent infidelity was considered adultery. The betrothal was followed some months later by the husband's taking his wife into his home, at which time normal married life began.1:19 A righteous man: as a devout observer of the Mosaic law, Joseph wished to break his union with someone whom he suspected of gross violation of the law. It is commonly said that the law required him to do so, but the texts usually given in support of that view, e.g., Dt 22:20–21 do not clearly pertain to Joseph's situation. Unwilling to expose her to shame: the penalty for proved adultery was death by stoning; cf. Dt 22:21–23.

1:20 The angel of the Lord: in the Old Testament a common designation of God in communication with a human being. In a dream: see Mt 2:13, 19,

22. These dreams may be meant to recall the dreams of Joseph, son of Jacob the patriarch (Gn 37:5–11, 19). A closer parallel is the dream of Amram, father of Moses, related by Josephus (*Antiquities* 2:212, 215–16). 1:21 Jesus: in first-century Judaism the Hebrew name Joshua (Greek *Iēsous*) meaning "Yahweh helps" was interpreted as "Yahweh saves."

1:23 God is with us: God's promise of deliverance to Judah in Isaiah's time is seen by Matthew as fulfilled in the birth of Jesus, in whom God is with his people. The name Emmanuel is alluded to at the end of the gospel where the risen Jesus assures his disciples of his continued presence, "...I am with you always, until the end of the age" (Mt 28:20).

1:25 Until she bore a son: the evangelist is concerned to emphasize that Joseph was not responsible for the conception of Jesus. The Greek word translated "until" does not imply normal marital conduct after Jesus' birth, nor does it exclude it.

In biblical times, one simply did not practice what was reserved for marriage. Rather than cause further shame and discontent among the community, Joseph was ready to divorce Mary, before he even married her. Then the power of God intervened. Joseph did exactly as was commanded of him in the dream. Joseph, a man of God, began to see the situation from the viewpoint of compassion. He was genuinely concerned for Mary's well being as an upstanding citizen. We can only wonder the course of Mary's life if Joseph did not obey God. Rather than leave Mary alone and afraid with onlookers wondering exactly who Jesus belonged to, Joseph embraced his role as foster father of the Son of God, himself. To this day, Joseph is applauded for upholding the righteousness of the church laws.

Reflection:

It all started with a single thought. Compassion. Then, it turned into many thoughts resembling a ball of twine. The only way to untangle the thoughts was to break it down even more. Are compassion and sympathy the same? No. Are compassion and empathy the same? No. Are sympathy and empathy the same? No. Then, exactly how do you differentiate among the three terms? After digging deeper, the ball of twine unwound. Let me share with you how I wrapped my mind around the term *compassion*. I started with the familiar: sympathy. Once I read about *sympathy*, my mind turned to the ANT (Automatic Negative Thought) I have about *sympathy*. Do NOT feel sorry for me; pity me. You see, I have a severe disability. Let me clarify: I have a severe UNSEEN disability. I know my limits and follow my doctor's orders, as best as humanly

Part 3: Human Virtues Close to My Heart

possible. If you see me NOT doing something, it's because it will have an adverse effect on my disability. Well, you may label me "lazy" for not doing something that you have no idea is beyond my limits. Then comes the day I let you in as part of my close circle of friends. I tell you about my disability. You no longer label me "lazy". At this point, you either begin to "pity" me or develop an attitude of "sympathy". No one enjoys being "pitied". It is a negative form of "sympathy". Pity expresses itself as "I'm glad I don't have to go through that" or "so glad it's you and not me". Sympathy is genuine concern and feeling another's pain. You are sorry that I hurt because you genuinely don't like to see another person hurt.

Then my mind began to focus on "empathy". Simply put, "empathy" means walking in another's shoes. This is not humanly possible. God made each person on earth unique. So, continuing with my example of my severe, unseen disability. There is no way you can begin to understand the emotions I go through on a daily basis related to what I can do, or rather what is detrimental to my health. Nor can you foresee the complexities of daily living that I navigate multiple times a day.

Finally, I clear the cobwebs away and "compassion" becomes clear. Compassion is meeting me right where I am and walking with me on my journey with love. You do not pretend to know how to respond to my daily limitations. You do not do these things for me. You cheer for me; encourage me; walk next to me, loving me through both my good and bad days. You are a constant positive source of energy in my life. I hope I do the same for you, as well. We cannot fully and totally carry each other's burdeons. Only Jesus can. But we can walk in Jesus' footsteps and have compassion for each other. It is in this way that compassion reminds me of the poem "Footprints in the Sand". Compassion also reminds me of Saint Joseph, Jesus' foster father, whom I wrote about in the actual reflection of this chapter.

Compassion

Question 1: Describe a time in your life that you followed what God asked of you in your heart, despite how it was viewed in society. In the end, how was your steadfastness in the Lord viewed?

Question 2: What are some positive qualities of compassion that you see in yourself? How do they help you grow?

Digging Deeper: Argue for or against these Biblical figures exhibiting the virtue of *compassion*:

- Ruth when she revealed to Naomi that Ruth would care for her (Ruth 1:6-18)

- Hosea when he realized his wife committed adultery (Hosea 3:1-5)

- The woman as she anointed Jesus' feet with the alabaster jar (Luke 7:36-50)

Part 3: Human Virtues Close to My Heart

Prayer: Let us conclude with the prayer referenced in my reflection.

Footprints in the Sand

One night I dreamed a dream.

As I was walking along the beach with my Lord. Across the dark sky flashed scenes from my life.

For each scene, I noticed two sets of footprints in the sand, One belonging to me and one to my Lord.

After the last scene of my life flashed before me, I looked back at the footprints in the sand.

I noticed that at many times along the path of my life, especially at the very lowest and saddest times,

there was only one set of footprints.

This really troubled me, so I asked the Lord about it. "Lord, you said once I decided to follow you,

You'd walk with me all the way.

But I noticed that during the saddest and most troublesome times of my life,

there was only one set of footprints.

I don't understand why, when I needed You the most, You would leave me." He whispered, "My precious child, I love you and will never leave you Never, ever, during your trials and testings.

When you saw only one set of footprints, It was then that I carried you."

Chapter 10

Perseverance

Defined in my own Words: continuance through all circumstances to be seen to the end of the process

Scripture:

> *Ephesians 6:18*
> "With all prayer and supplication, pray at every opportunity in the Spirit. To that end, be watchful with all perseverance and supplication for all the holy ones"

> *John 15:13*
> "[a]No one has greater love than this, to lay down one's life for one's friends."

Catechism of the Catholic Church:

> *#2753*
> "In the battle of prayer we must confront erroneous conceptions of prayer, various currents of thought, and our own experience of failure. We must respond with humility, trust, and perseverance to these temptations which cast doubt on the usefulness or even the possibility of prayer."

Sponsored by: Saint Monica, mother of Saint Augustine of Hippo
Patron Saint of: Difficult Marriages, Wives, & Abuse Victims
Feast Day: August 27

PART 3: HUMAN VIRTUES CLOSE TO MY HEART

Insight in Saint Monica's Words:

"Nothing is far from God."

"Son, nothing in this world now affords me delight. I do not know what there is now left for me to do or why I am still here, all my hopes in this world being now fulfilled."—Confessions by Saint Augustine

Real Lives, Real Stories:

The word "defeat" was never a part of Dad Thomas' vocabulary. Not when he was a toddler growing up on the farm. Not as a young boy learning in school. Not as the eldest sibling of five. Not as a construction worker building the Kansas highways as his first trade.

Upon returning to his apartment after a visit home, Dad Thomas, at age 22, suffered a stroke. His roommate was the one to discover him, a day later.

Defeat was not in Dad's vocabulary as he persevered through the physical therapy in healing from his stroke. Though Dad never regained the use of his right side, he found other ways to overcome and soar to all God created him to be.

As Dad learned to adapt from the right-side paralysis, he went to school and became an accountant. He then rose in the ranks of the Internal Revenue Service to become District Director. He kept his eyes on the prize: Jesus.

Dad married and settled in Fremont, NE. There, two children were born. Defeat was never in in their vocabulary either. Still isn't.

As District Director, his family moved every three years: Little Rock, AR; Plano, TX; Nashville, TN; Jacksonville, FL; and Wichita, KS. Setting up a new home and the kids making friends had its challenges, but as I said, "defeat" was not in their vocabulary. Mom's first task upon each move was to become an active member of the Catholic Church closest to each residence. Dad had a strong faith and belief in God. He was an ardent church attendee until years later when health problems prevented him from attending. Their children were raised in the faith.

So, what exactly did I see in Dad that he gets the honor of my real-life example of perseverance? Dad was an exemplary worker, always striving for the best. He took a chance each time he was offered a promotion. He rose to the occasion and ran the districts with a firm purpose. Most of all, he never once felt sorry for himself. Ever. It is through my difficulties that I talk to Dad. I know that he made it through some tough times. He's now on the other side praying and loving from above as his family perseveres through this life, as he did. With that, what could go wrong?

Reflection:

"They" say a picture is worth 1000 words. When I look at a picture of St. Monica, it is hard not to notice the effects of praying without ceasing (wrinkled hands & face; the intense, see-right-through-you stare; hands clasped together tightly). Based on the picture, Saint Monica looks to be approaching age 90. In reality, Saint Monica died at the age of 56.

Suddenly, the camera comes into focus with a single lens. Saint Monica persevered in prayer with God day after day after

Part 3: Human Virtues Close to My Heart

day. Saint Monica incorporated constant prayer with a side of hope garnished with believing the unbelievable. Saint Monica witnessed through uttering the most faint cry several times daily that her husband and mother-in-law come to know Jesus. Indeed they did. Saint Monica was an eye witness as her husband, Patricius, and her mother-in-law committed their lives to Jesus. It was roughly a year before the death of her husband.

But that's not all. Upon the death of Patricius, their son, Augustine, left the Catholic Church. This caused Saint Monica grief and angst that only a mother would know. Saint Monica knew the formula: praying around the clock. Saint Monica was faithful to God for a total of 17 years, pleading for Augustine to return to the faith. Through divine intervention with the help of Saint Ambrose, Saint Monica saw the fruit of her prayers: Augustine returned to the Catholic Church. It was at this time that Saint Monica told her son, Augustine,

> "Son, nothing in this world now affords me delight. I do not know what there is now left for me to do or why I am still here, all my hopes in this world being now fulfilled."—Confessions by Saint Augustine

It was shortly after Augustine returned to the Catholic faith that Saint Monica expired her last breath. Her life on earth was complete. Her life as a Saint of God had just begun.

> **Question 1:** Describe a situation in your life when you prayed like you have never prayed before. What were the fruits of that prayer?

Perseverance

Question 2: How can you extend the olive branch to someone who is hesitant of living countercultural to what the world offers us today?

Digging Deeper: Argue for or against these Biblical figures exhibiting the virtue of *perseverance*:

- Zechariah upon hearing he would have a son and name him John (Luke 1:68-79)

- Zacchaeus climbing the tree to see Jesus (Luke 19:1-10)

- The bleeding woman upon touching Jesus' cloak (Luke 8:43-48)

Prayer: Dear Lord Jesus, In my darkest of nights and the dawn of tomorrows, help me recognize the gift of today. Teach me and guide me in Your ways in order to continue to be all that you have called me to be.

Chapter 11

Authenticity

Defined in my own Words: being yourself; confidence in self but not to the point of bragging
Scripture:

> *Hebrews 13:18*
> "Pray for us, for we are confident that we have a clear conscience, wishing to act rightly in every respect."

> *Proverbs 3:26*
> "For the LORD will be your confidence, and will keep your foot from the snare."

> *Philippians 1:25-26*
> "And this I know with confidence, that I shall remain and continue in the service of all of you for your progress and joy in the faith, 26 so that your boasting in Christ Jesus may abound on account of me when I come to you again.

> *Thessalonians 3:4*
> "We are confident of you in the Lord that what we instruct you, you [both] are doing and will continue to do."

> *1 John 5:14*
> "And we have this confidence in him, that if we ask anything according to his will, he hears us."

AUTHENTICITY

Catechism of the Catholic Church:

#2504-#2505
"You shall not bear false witness against your neighbor" (*Ex* 20:16). Christ's disciples have "put on the new man, created after the likeness of God in true righteousness and holiness" (*Eph* 4:24). Truth or truthfulness is the virtue which consists in showing oneself true in deeds and truthful in words, and guarding against duplicity, dissimulation, and hypocrisy."

#2472
"The duty of Christians to take part in the life of the Church impels them to act as *witnesses of the Gospel* and of the obligations that flow from it. This witness is a transmission of the faith in words and deeds. Witness is an act of justice that establishes the truth or makes it known. [269] All Christians by the example of their lives and the witness of their word, wherever they live, have an obligation to manifest the new man which they have put on in Baptism and to reveal the power of the Holy Spirit by whom they were strengthened at Confirmation." [270]

[269] Cf. Mt 18:16.
[270] AG 11.

#2465
"The Old Testament attests that *God is the source of all truth*. His Word is truth. His Law is truth. His "faithfulness endures to all generations." [255] Since God is "true," the members of his people are called to live in the truth." [256]

[255] Ps 119:90; Cf. Prov 8:7; 2 Sam 7:28; Ps 119:142; Lk 1:50.
[256] Rom 3:4; Cf. Ps 119:30.

Sponsored by: Father Emil Kapaun—Saint to Be
Patron Saint of: Yet to be determined
Feast Day: Yet to be determined
Insight in Father Kapaun's Words:

> "Pray hard, receive the sacraments frequently, and above all give good example."

Part 3: Human Virtues Close to My Heart

"Out of suffering have emerged the strongest souls. . .."

"And when it seems impossible, remember that as he was carried away to the dying place, Fr. Kapaun told "his boys:" ". . .When I get up there, I'll say a prayer for all of you."

Real lives, Real Stories:

Word	Defined in my Own Words	Synonyms	Antynoms	Sentence Example
Authenticity	walk the walk and talk the talk; promises kept	credibility reliability trustworthyness	inaccuracy impure	On stage she looked radiant with experience; authenticity in the making.
Genuine	being yourself with no fear of what others think of you	real absolute certain	doubtful questionable	With a genuine heart, he helped his ailing grandma to the car.
Honesty	what you see is what you get; telling it all no matter the feedback	confidence sincerity faithful	corrupt immoral	As he proposed to his girlfriend, his demeanor showed nothing but honesty of his love for her.
Integrity	giving the benefit of the doubt; keeping your word	honor upright straightforward	deceit dishonesty	Her doctor's knowledge is impeccable, yet his bedside manner is seriously lacking in integrity.
Truthful	keeping it real regardless of consequences	accurate believable candid	devious false	The child finally opened up to his counselor, telling every truthful detail about how his dad behaves at home.

Authenticity

Authenticity is a unique word. Authenticity can be compared to the following words: genuine, honesty, integrity, and truthful. Authenticity is not only talking the talk, but also walking the walk. Actions speak louder than words. We must allow our actions to speak even more so than our words. Authenticity also means you keep your promises. For example, if you say you are going to be at your Holy Hour, you need to go there. If you opt out, you are not keeping your promise. When you keep your promise word for word you remain credible and reliable as well as trustworthy. Authenticity is all that and more. Others will see that you are a person of authenticity. You keep your promises. Every one of them.

I could tell right away that Daniel is a man of his word. After a 2-year vacancy, the house next door to us was purchased at a phenomenal price due to the fact that substantial repairs were needed. Daniel's family worked diligently transforming the house into their home. As I watched this process, a single thought formed in my head. Perhaps Daniel is the right person to help us remodel our kitchen, entryway, and bathrooms. I continued to observe this labor of love that only homeowners understand. What stood out the most was Daniel's effort and time management skills.

Within a 24-hour period, Daniel had his remodeling proposal to us. We graciously accepted his proposal. We worked our schedules and payments according to a payment plan that the four of us agreed upon. It was during the remodeling process that the bond among the four of us grew to a deeper level.

One quality about Daniel became self-evident as the four of us became closer. Daniel is not afraid to voice his faults, especially when doing so shows growth in his love of God. One example of this is the motorcycle accident. Daniel took time out of his schedule to share his faith journey with us. Eight years ago, Daniel was "showing off" while riding his motorcycle. The result of "showing off" was a serious wreck that nearly cost Daniel his right arm. Though Daniel's right arm was salvaged, it would never function the same again. This is one example of authenticity. Daniel never denied how the wreck occurred or the fact that saving his right arm means struggling daily with pain. Add to that the fact that

Part 3: Human Virtues Close to My Heart

Daniel remodeled our home not once complaining of pain. There is nothing more authentic than watching someone who struggles DAILY with pain to make you realize that each of God's creations does, in fact, struggle in one way or another.

Another trait of authenticity is teaching someone without putting him/her down. Daniel continues to take time out of his packed schedule to model for us simple home repair jobs, which are not our forte. He patiently teaches us with a step-by-step hands on mode. This hands-on teaching mode is second nature for Daniel. Daniel has successfully, and will continue to, teach his oldest two children more than just home repair lessons. Daniel models every aspect of learning for his older children (ages 8 & 3). Daniel's wife just had a baby (age 7 weeks); her first, Daniel's third. Daniel is a completely relaxed father. He is now teaching baby as he did his older two. Even better is the fact that his oldest two children are teaching their baby sister as Daddy taught them.

This persona of confident authenticity, rather than episodically egotistical, radiates for all to see. Authenticity does not stop there. Daniel takes it a step further. Daniel listens with an empathetic ear at any given time. Not only does he listen, but days later, Daniel asks follow-up questions about the topics at hand. We cover a wide array of topics: medical, political, financial, spiritual, etc. I thank God daily that our families are friends and that we are a support system for each other.

Reflection:

So, what is it about Daniel (and his wife) that makes him legit? Or for that matter, how does an almost canonized saint (Father Emil Kapuan) live and move his very being so in tune authentically that it can be emulated by others (e.g. Daniel) for years to come? I mean, emulated in a way that another saint is identified for possible canonization? "10 [a]For the Son of Man has come to seek and to save what was lost." (Luke 19:10)

19:10 This verse sums up for Luke his depiction of the role of Jesus as savior in this gospel.

AUTHENTICITY

Daniel listens and provides input without passing judgment. Daniel is also a realist, in that he recognizes life is a contact sport. As Daniel models by example, he is a godly man and relies on his faith in God to overcome adversity by authenticity. Family comes a close second to God. With Daniel, what you see is what you get. That is what makes Daniel legit.

In comparison, Father Emil Kapuan brought Jesus, Himself, to those WWII servicemen and servicewomen each time he prepared the hood of his jeep to be the makeshift altar used for DAILY Mass for those who might not see the end of the day at hand. With sincere love for those in need, Father Kapuan continued to serve authentically from the heart. This is love in action; Father Kapuan was legit. Father Kapuan brought Jesus to many during the uncertainty of the very real war going on amongst all on the battlefield. Father Kapaun had his eyes focused on the prize: saving souls by making the body and blood available to all those in need.

Father Kapaun had a similar experience to Jesus, himself. There was no place Father Kapaun wanted to be other than with God. Father Kapaun found joy as an altar server. That insurmountable joy was the prelude to Father Kapaun entering the seminary and becoming a diocesan priest Upon his ordination, Father Kapaun was assigned to his hometown parish in Pilsen, Kansas. It was during this time that Father Kapaun felt the parishioners lack of trust to confide in him. This also happened to Jesus each time he would return home to Nazareth. Neither one was welcome in his hometown. It was for this reason that Father Kapaun began the path to be a chaplain in World War II. Father Kapaun let God mold him and use him where God saw fit. So, yes, it is possible to grow up in a small town and make a serious impact amongst fellow believers. What set Father Kapaun apart from that was that he, himself, actually became a prisoner of war, which led to his death. Father Kapaun gave his life by the means of pneumonia and starvation as a prisoner of war. The path to sainthood is a lengthy process and in time, Father Emil Kapaun will be counted as an official saint in the Catholic Church amongst those fellow servants of God.

Part 3: Human Virtues Close to My Heart

As a side story, my paternal grandparents met in Herington, KS, a mere 16 miles north of Pilsen, KS. During their courtship and early years of marriage, my grandparents would drive to Pilsen for Saturday evening Mass and dances that would follow in the parish hall. I must admit, I do crack a smile knowing that my grandparents crossed paths with a saint to be.

Question 1: Which one of these words describes you: authentic, genuine, honest, integrity, truthful? Provide three examples of why you chose that word.

Question 2: Who is the one person that you trust most to hold you accountable to remain authentic? How does this person help you to become a better Catholic Christian?

Digging Deeper: Argue for or against these Biblical figures exhibiting the virtue of *authenticity*:

- Matthew's conversion of less taxes, more God (Matthew 9:9-13)

AUTHENTICITY

- The Widow's offering to God (Mark 12:41-44)

- Onesimus upon making it right with God (Philemon 8-21)

Prayer: Here I am, Lord. Take me now. Wrap me in the arms of your love through the good and the bad. Please provide me many, many memories of the good times so that they soothe me through the tough times. Know that I am your servant, willing You to lead me here on Earth. Thank you for calling me yours. Amen Jesus.

Chapter 12

Purposefulness

Defined in my own Words: focusing on the project at hand and having the drive to finish it
Scripture:

> *Romans 8:28*
> "[a]We know that all things work for good for those who love God,[b] who are called according to his purpose."

> *Matthew 7:12*
> "Do to others whatever you would have them do to you. This is the law and the prophets."

> *Galatians 5:13-14, 22, 25*
> "For you were called for freedom, brothers. But do not use this freedom as an opportunity for the flesh; rather, serve[a] one another through love. For the whole law is fulfilled in one statement, namely, "You shall love your neighbor as yourself."[b]
>
> the fruit of the Spirit is love, joy, peace, patience, kindness, generosity, faithfulness, gentleness, self-control.
>
> If we live in the Spirit, let us also follow the Spirit."

Purposefulness

Catechism of the Catholic Church:

> *#1490*
> "The movement of return to God, called conversion and repentance, entails sorrow for and abhorrence of sins committed, and the firm purpose of sinning no more in the future. Conversion touches the past and the future and is nourished by hope in God's mercy."

Sponsored by: Saint Faustina Kowalska
Patron Saint of: Divine Mercy
Feast Day: October 5
Insight in Saint Faustina's Words:

> "God is very generous and does not deny His grace to anyone. Indeed he gives more than what we ask of Him. Faithfulness to the inspirations of the Holy Spirit-that is the shortest route."

> "Entrust everything to Me and do nothing on your own, and you will always have great freedom of spirit."

Real Lives, Real Stories:

Coincidence? I think not. It was purely God's will that three of His saints ministered in Krakow, Poland, to those most in need. Though it was not recognizable at that time in history, these three saints made history. Three prophecies (one from each saint) show God's master plan in action.

The first is Saint Pope John Paul II. His prophecy was that all persons on fire for our Lord will pass through great trials. It is through the great trials that God is asking us to live countercultural to what the world offers. This takes great strength in God and a strong support system who understands the concept and holds those accountable for living this lifestyle.

The second is Saint Maximilian Kolbe. His prophecy is that Satan is ever present urging all persons to turn away from Jesus. We must stay steadfast, not falling for the pleasures of this world, especially when it breeds conflict. What makes this prophecy

Part 3: Human Virtues Close to My Heart

unique is that Mary the Mother of God is requesting that these persons consecrate themselves to herself to aid in defeating Satan. One result from this prophecy is that Saint Maximilian Kolbe traded places with a family man due to be executed during WWII. Yes, this saint of God took the killing that freed a family man from the snares of war.

The third is Saint Faustina Kowalska. She was asked by God Himself to let the world know of Jesus and his divine mercy for all souls. Saint Faustina's prophecy is found in her *Diary*.

#965 "Jesus looked at me and said, "Souls perish in spite of My bitter Passion. I am giving them the last hope of salvation; that is, the Feast of My Mercy. If they will not adore My mercy, they will perish for all eternity.

Secretary of My mercy, write, tell souls about this great mercy of Mine, because the awful day, the day of My justice, is near."

Now, fast forward to the year 2000. Saint John Paul II reinvigorated the concept of "divine mercy" and after the proper inquiry, he elevated Faustina Kowalska to sainthood.

Though I have studied these three saints, I did not realize until recently that Saint John Paul II, Saint Maximilian Kolbe, and Saint Faustina trod the streets of Krakow, Poland, during the same era, affecting millions, not even realizing each other's input. They were each embedded in their purpose set forth by God that they never took their gaze off of Jesus to see the exact progress made by others during the 20th century.

Reflection:

When I study about purposefulness, this picture of Jesus comes to mind:

This is the exact image Saint Faustina was to make known to the world about Jesus' never-ending mercy. After reading Saint Faustina's full account of this request, her energy and drive to fulfill this purpose Jesus asked of her increased one hundred-fold. This excerpt of Jesus' request comes from Saint Faustina's Diary:

"# 1074 When I went for adoration, I heard these words: My beloved daughter, write down these words, that today My Heart has rested in this convent [the Cracow house]. Tell the world about My mercy and My love. The flames of mercy are burning me. I desire to pour them out upon human souls. Oh, what pain they cause Me when they do not want to accept them! My daughter, do whatever is within your power to spread devotion to My mercy. I will make up for what you lack. Tell aching mankind to snuggle close to My merciful Heart, and I will fill it with peace. Tell [all people], My daughter, that I am Love and Mercy itself. When a

Part 3: Human Virtues Close to My Heart

soul approaches Me with trust, I fill it with such an abundance of graces that it cannot contain them within itself, but radiates them to other souls.

1075 Souls who spread the honor of My mercy I shield through their entire lives as a tender mother her infant, and at the hour of death I will not be a Judge for them, but the merciful Savior. (21) At that last hour, a soul has nothing with which to defend itself except My mercy. Happy is the soul that during its lifetime immersed itself in the Fountain of Mercy, because justice will have no hold on it. "

So, how can I use the purpose God has given me for the betterment of all. Simply by these two words: Speak Life. Exactly how is this accomplished?

Just by taking action based upon the lyrics to "Speak Life" by tobymac

"Speak Life"
Tobymac

Some days, life feels perfect. Other days it just ain't workin.
The good, the bad, the right, the wrong And everything in between.

Though it's crazy, amazing
We can turn a heart with the words we say.
Mountains crumble with every syllable.
Hope can live or die

So speak Life, speak Life.
To the deadest darkest night.
Speak life, speak Life.
When the sun won't shine and you don't know why.
Look into the eyes of the brokenhearted;
Watch them come alive as soon as you speak hope,
You speak love, you speak. . .
You speak Life, (oh oh oh oh oh oh) You speak Life. (oh oh oh oh oh oh)

Purposefulness

Some days the tongue gets twisted;
Other days my thoughts just fall apart.
I do, I don't, I will, I won't, It's like I'm drowning in the deep.

Well it's crazy to imagine,
Words from our lips as the arms of compassion,
Mountains crumble with every syllable.
Hope can live or die.

So speak Life, speak Life.
To the deadest darkest night.
Speak life, speak Life

Question 1: Describe a time when you were the recipient of the concept of "Speak Life". Explain a situation where you "Spoke Life" to another person.

Question 2: Whom do you turn to when you need to be spoken to with life? Why?

Digging Deeper: Argue for or against these Biblical figures exhibiting the virtue of *purposefulness*:

- Simeon upon seeing Baby Jesus (Luke 2:25-35)

PART 3: HUMAN VIRTUES CLOSE TO MY HEART

- Jabez's earnest prayer to God (1 Chronicles 4:9-10)

- The Wisemen who visited Baby Jesus in the manger (Matthew 2:1-12)

Prayer: Dear Lord Jesus, the first words God spoke were those bringing life to every living being. Please continue to guide me in all that I think, do, and say. Let the words off my lips bring life to all. Amen Jesus.

Appendix 1
Lincoln's "Failures"?

BELOW IS ONE VERSION of the so-called "Lincoln failures" list, shown in bold type. It's often used to inspire people to overcome life's difficulties with Lincoln as a model. Then look at the right column with other facts from Lincoln's pre-presidential life. History professor Lucas Morel compiled this comparison from the Chronology in *Selected Speeches and Writings/Lincoln* by Don E. Fehrenbacher, ed., 1992.

YEAR	FAILURES or SETBACKS	SUCCESSES
1832	Lost job Defeated for state legislature	Elected company captain of Illinois militia in Black Hawk War
1833	Failed in business	Appointed postmaster of New Salem, Illinois Appointed deputy surveyor of Sangamon County
1834		Elected to Illinois state legislature
1835	Sweetheart died	
1836	Had nervous breakdown	Re-elected to Illinois state legislature (running first in his district) Received license to practice law in Illinois state courts
1837		Led Whig delegation in moving Illinois state capital from Vandalia to Springfield Became law partner of John T. Stuart

Appendix 1

YEAR	FAILURES or SETBACKS	SUCCESSES
1838	Defeated for Speaker	Nominated for Illinois House Speaker by Whig caucus Re-elected to Illinois House (running first in his district) Served as Whig floor leader
1839		Chosen presidential elector by first Whig convention Admitted to practice law in U.S. Circuit Court
1840		Argues first case before Illinois Supreme Court Re-elected to Illinois state legislature
1841		Established new law practice with Stephen T. Logan
1842		Admitted to practice law in U.S. District Court
1843	Defeated for nomination for Congress	
1844		Established own law practice with William H. Herndon as junior partner
1846		Elected to Congress
1848	Lost renomination	(Chose not to run for Congress, abiding by rule of rotation among Whigs.)
1849	Rejected for land officer	Admitted to practice law in U.S. Supreme Court Declined appointment as secretary and then as governor of Oregon Territory
1854	Defeated for U.S. Senate	Elected to Illinois state legislature (but declined seat to run for U.S. Senate)
1856	Defeated for nomination for Vice President	
1858	Again defeated for U.S. Senate	
1860		Elected President

Appendix 2

Emancipation Proclamation Text

The Emancipation Proclamation
January 1, 1863

A Transcription By the President of the United States of America:

A Proclamation

Whereas, on the twenty-second day of September, in the year of our Lord one thousand eight hundred and sixty-two, a proclamation was issued by the President of the United States, containing, among other things, the following, to wit:

"That on the first day of January, in the year of our Lord one thousand eight hundred and sixty-three, all persons held as slaves within any State or designated part of a State, the people whereof shall then be in rebellion against the United States, shall be then, thenceforward, and forever free; and the Executive Government of the United States, including the military and naval authority thereof, will recognize and maintain the freedom of such persons, and will do no act or acts to repress such persons, or any of them, in any efforts they may make for their actual freedom.

Appendix 2

"That the Executive will, on the first day of January aforesaid, by proclamation, designate the States and parts of States, if any, in which the people thereof, respectively, shall then be in rebellion against the United States; and the fact that any State, or the people thereof, shall on that day be, in good faith, represented in the Congress of the United States by members chosen thereto at elections wherein a majority of the qualified voters of such State shall have participated, shall, in the absence of strong countervailing testimony, be deemed conclusive evidence that such State, and the people thereof, are not then in rebellion against the United States."

Now, therefore I, Abraham Lincoln, President of the United States, by virtue of the power in me vested as Commander-in-Chief, of the Army and Navy of the United States in time of actual armed rebellion against the authority and government of the United States, and as a fit and necessary war measure for suppressing said rebellion, do, on this first day of January, in the year of our Lord one thousand eight hundred and sixty-three, and in accordance with my purpose so to do publicly proclaimed for the full period of one hundred days, from the day first above mentioned, order and designate as the States and parts of States wherein the people thereof respectively, are this day in rebellion against the United States, the following, to wit:

Arkansas, Texas, Louisiana, (except the Parishes of St. Bernard, Plaquemines, Jefferson, St. John, St. Charles, St. James Ascension, Assumption, Terrebonne, Lafourche, St. Mary, St. Martin, and Orleans, including the City of New Orleans) Mississippi, Alabama, Florida, Georgia, South Carolina, North Carolina, and Virginia, (except the forty-eight counties designated as West Virginia, and also the counties of Berkley, Accomac, Northampton, Elizabeth City, York, Princess Ann, and Norfolk, including the cities of Norfolk and Portsmouth[)], and which excepted parts, are for the present, left precisely as if this proclamation were not issued.

And by virtue of the power, and for the purpose aforesaid, I do order and declare that all persons held as slaves within said

Emancipation Proclamation Text

designated States, and parts of States, are, and henceforward shall be free; and that the Executive government of the United States, including the military and naval authorities thereof, will recognize and maintain the freedom of said persons.

And I hereby enjoin upon the people so declared to be free to abstain from all violence, unless in necessary self-defence; and I recommend to them that, in all cases when allowed, they labor faithfully for reasonable wages.

And I further declare and make known, that such persons of suitable condition, will be received into the armed service of the United States to garrison forts, positions, stations, and other places, and to man vessels of all sorts in said service.

And upon this act, sincerely believed to be an act of justice, warranted by the Constitution, upon military necessity, I invoke the considerate judgment of mankind, and the gracious favor of Almighty God.

In witness whereof, I have hereunto set my hand and caused the seal of the United States to be affixed.

Done at the City of Washington, this first day of January, in the year of our Lord one thousand eight hundred and sixty three, and of the Independence of the United States of America the eighty-seventh.

By the President: ABRAHAM LINCOLN
WILLIAM H. SEWARD, Secretary of State.

Bibliography

Chapter 1: Faith

Maalouf, J. (2001). *Mother Teresa: Essential Writings*. Maryknoll, NY: Orbis Books.

Evinger, A. (2016, September 4). http://www.ncregister.com/site/print/50752 "The Unlikely Friendship Between Mother Teresa and Princess Diana". Retrieved from URL

Chapter 2: Hope

Anonymous. Quote "Don't EVER give up!"
https://www.stjude.org/
http://www.quotegarden.com/hope.html
Moore, K. R. (2001). *An Hour with Saint Jude*. Liguori, MO: Liguori Publications.

Chapter 3: Charity

Saint Therese of Lisieux. (2010). *The Story of a Soul*. Charlotte, N.C.: Tan Books.

Chapter 4: Prudence

http://sjohio.org/assets/templates/mycustom/ethereal/files/lesson/holyspirit/Lesson27ATheCardinalVirtueof%20Prudence.pdf

Richert, S.P. (2017, July 11). The cardinal virtues:the four hinges of the moral life. Retrieved from https://www.thoughtco.com/the-cardinal-virtues-542142

Richert, S.P. (2016, April 17). Prudence: a cardinal virtue: Doing what's good and avoiding what's evil. Retrieved from: https://www.thoughtco.com/prudence-a-cardinal-virtue-542128

Bibliography

Catholic Online. (n.d.) Saints & Angels: St. Thomas More. Retrieved August 30, 2017, from http://www.catholic.org/saints/saint.php?saint_id=324

The Catholic Gentleman. (n.d.) St. Thomas More: A saint for the persecuted church. Retrieved on September 6, 2017, from https://www.catholicgentleman.net/2016/07/st-thomas-saint-persecuted-church/

Dynamic Youth Alive. A man for our season: the virtues of thomas more and their relevancy to our times. (n.d.) Retrieved on September 6, 2017, from http://dynamicyouthalive.blogspot.com/2013/04/a-man-for-our-season-virtues-of-thomas.html

That Virtue Lesson Series. Lesson 27 – The Cardinal virtue of prudence. (n.d.) Retrieved on September 1, 2017 from http://www.thatresourcesite.com

Hodges. S. (2014, June 17). Vatican Radio. Pope Francis to Italian magistrates: Be prudent, impartial and models of morality. Retrieved from http://en.radiovaticana.va/news/2014/06/17/pope_francis_addresses_italian_magistrates/1101867#

Martin, I.S. (2017, January 25). Crux: Taking the Catholic Pulse. Opus Dei leaders describe warm relationship with Pope Francis. Retrieved from https://cruxnow.com/global-church/2017/01/25/opus-dei-leaders-describe-warm-relationship-pope-francis/

Saint Josemaria Escriva. Pope Francis describes prayer as a way to seek counsel from God. Retrieved on September 7, 2017 from http://www.josemariaescriva.info/article/pope-francis-describes-prayer-as-a-way-to-seek-counsel-from-god

Christian Art Gifts. (2013). *Keep calm and pray.* China: Christian Art Gifts.

Chapter 5: Justice

Ovile, R. (2015, October 21). The relationship of mercy and justice according to St. Thomas Aquinas. Retrieved from https://gloria.tv/article/4aFCMyrXocDf4u7jLtSUeecM6

Gates Jr., H. L. (2014, January 27). Did Lincoln really free the slaves?. Retrieved from http://www.theroot.com/did-lincoln-really-free-the-slaves-1790874318

Adams, A. H. (2013, February 5). Why did Lincoln free the slaves? Retrieved from http://www.historynet.com/why-did-lincoln-finally-free-the-slaves.htm

Pruitt, S. (2012, September 21). 5 Things You May Not Know About Lincoln, Slavery and Emancipation. Retrieved from http://www.history.com/news/5-things-you-may-not-know-about-lincoln-slavery-and-emancipation

School of Faith. (2014). The standard of happiness: Virtue and Catholic morality. Holly's notes and class handbook for study.

Bibliography

Coopersmith, W. (2013). Thomas Aquinas on the role of government. Retrieved November 3, 2017 from http://www.valuesandcapitalism.com/thomas-aquinas-on-the-role-of-government/

Jurisprudence by PBT. Saint Thomas Aquinas 4 categories of law. (2011). Retrieved November 3, 2017, from http://quillsforthewritingheartjurisprudence.blogspot.com/2014/11/stthomas-aquinas-4-categories-of-law.html

Morel, L. (2017). Lincoln's failures? Retrieved November 4, 2017 from http://www.abrahamlincolnonline.org/lincoln/education/failures.htm

Burlingame, M. (n.d.). Abraham Lincoln: Campaigns and elections. Retrieved November 4, 2017, from https://millercenter.org/president/lincoln/campaigns-and-elections

Chapter 6: Fortitude

Zanini, R. I. (2013). *Bakhita: From Slave to Saint*. San Francisco, CA: Ignatius Press.

Chapter 7: Temperance

Englebert, O. (1965). *St. Francis of Assisi: A Biography*. Ann Arbor, MI: Franciscan Herald Press.

Chapter 8: Patience

Weninger, Father F. X. (2016, November 19). Saint Elizabeth of Hungary, Widow. Retrieved from https://reginamag.com/saint-elizabeth-of-hungary-widow/

Body theology. St. Elizabeth of Hungary. Retrieved from http://www.itmonline.org/bodytheology/stelizabeth.htm on October 16, 2017.

Catholic Online. (n.d.) Saints & Angels: St. Elizabeth of Hungary. Retrieved October 10, 2017, from http://www.catholic.org/saints/saint.php?saint_id=45

Chapter 9: Compassion

Catholic online. Saints & Angels: Saint Joseph. Retrieved August 12, 2017, from http://www.catholic.org/saints/saint.php?saint_id=4

Rozario, S. (2015, March 19). St. Joseph: Patron of the Universe and Social Justice. Retrieved from http://www.holycrosscongregation.org/news/st-joseph-patron-of-the-universe-and-social-justice/

Bibliography

Operation Meditation. Sympathy vs. Empathy vs. Compassion. Retrieved August 12, 2017, from http://operationmeditation.com/discover/sympathy-vs-empathy-vs-compassion/

Chapter 10: Perseverence

Saint Augustine (1961). Confessions. England: Penguin Books. http://www.catholic.org/saints/saint.php?saint_id=1

Chapter 11: Authenticity

Wenzl, R. & Heying, T. (2013). *The Miracle of Father Kapun: Priest, Soldier, and Korean War Hero*. San Francisco, CA: Ignatius Press.

Maher, W. L. (1997). *A Shepherd in Combat Boots: Chaplain Emil Kapun of the 1st Calvary Division*. Shippensburg, PY: Burd Street Press.

Catholic Diocese of Wichita. Father Kapaun Cause. Retrieved September 24, 2017, from http://catholicdioceseofwichita.org/2nd-seminarian-resources/sr-celibacy/lazarus-newsletters/office-documents-1/father-kapaun-cause-1?format=html.

Several Categories. Documents available through this website: The Story of Father Kapaun Booklet; Fr. Kapaun Path to Sainthood; The Year of Fr. Kapaun; VFW Magazine-- Fr. Emil Kapaun Story.

Watner, A. (n.d.). Retrieved on September 24, 2017, from http://www.roman-catholic-saints.com/father-kapaun.html

StrengthsMining: Tapping into your strengths for a better life. Honesty, authenticity, integrity. (n.d.). Retrieved on September 23, 2017, from http://www.strengthsmining.com/via-strengths/courage/honesty-authenticity-integrity/

Admin. (2014, March 26). Honesty, authenticity, and genuineness: Are you up for the challenge?. Retrieved from http://harvestinghappiness.com/honesty-authenticity-genuineness-challenge/

Chapter 12: Purposefulness

Saint Maria Faustina Kowalska. (2013). *Divine Mercy in My Soul: Diary of Saint Maria Faustina Kowalska*. Stockbridge, MA: Marian Press.

Ignatius Press. (2013). *Three Lives-One Vision-No Limits: Ocean of Mercy*. All Rights Reserved. Ignatius Press.

BIBLIOGRAPHY

General Resources

Gaitley, M. E. (2016). *33 Days to Merciful Love*. Stockbridge, MA: Marian Press.
Guardini, R. (1987). *Learning the Virtues that lead you to God*. Manchester, NH: Sophia Institute Press.
Craughwell, T. J. (2011). *Patron Saints*. Huntington, IN: Our Sunday Visitor Publishing Division.

www.ingramcontent.com/pod-product-compliance
Lightning Source LLC
Chambersburg PA
CBHW070509090426
42735CB00012B/2703